BILATERAL
MONETARY
THEORY

Also by Thomas Bewley Haran

THE MONETARY ANALYSIS

BILATERAL MONETARY THEORY

THOMAS BEWLEY HARAN

JANUS PUBLISHING COMPANY
London, England

First published in Great Britain 1998
by Janus Publishing Company Limited,
Edinburgh House, 19 Nassau Street,
London W1N 7RE

www.januspublishing.co.uk

**A CIP catalogue record for this book
is available from the British Library**

ISBN 1 85756 389 1

Phototypeset in 10.5 on 12 Times
by Keyboard Services, Luton, Beds

Cover design Creative Line

Printed and bound in Great Britain by
Antony Rowe Ltd, Chippenham, Wiltshire

Contents

Introduction

The Mystery of the Vanishing Money Supply

The economics profession and the monetary authorities maintain that cash and deposits are purchasing power, or, to use their term, 'liquidity'. Here, however, is a mystery.

Suppose that Britain became a cashless society and that the notes and coin in circulation were paid into accounts with banks and building societies. Savers would increase their deposits, while borrowers would reduce their indebtedness.

The money supply (taken here as cash plus deposits) would fall! Moreover, since the main suppliers of goods and services, such as industry, shops, etc, are bank borrowers, the fall would be substantial. Where then would the difference in purchasing power have gone?

The cash would be returned to the Bank of England and, in redemption, exchanged for the government securities presently held in cover of the note and coin issues. Bankers' Deposits at the Bank would not, therefore, increase, so the solution does not lie there.

Under a different banking system, an American one, overdrawn positions are not permitted and loans are credited instead to deposit accounts. Now, if this system were in use, the cash would be paid entirely into creditor accounts and it would appear that the money supply was not affected. The plot thickens!

There is, of course, a solution to the mystery, but it is not to be found in traditional monetary theory. Such theory is suspect and a question must rest over the extent.

Is this a major or a minor matter?

Unfortunately, it is very much a major one. Everyone knows how to use the monetary system, but, owing to false teaching, there is little or no understanding of the effects of the trading activity, the intricacies of the settlement procedures, the financing of the supply of goods and services and the ways in which the economy could be managed in order to eliminate inflation, cause prices to fall and provide full employment.

My methods

During the course of my banking career, I became unhappy with the teaching, (1) that banks create credit, and hence money, by lending, and (2) that thereafter, apart from open market operations by the monetary authorities, it circulated from hand to hand.

I thought it must be possible to determine whether these concepts were true or false by examining the transactions which make up modern economies, and the means by which they are settled. It did not matter to me how the results came out as long as I could justify them.

In the event, the concepts proved to be false and my findings are in stark contrast to those obtained by economists using traditional methods, such as building on the views of their predecessors or by making deductions based on interpretations of empirical evidence. It transpired that virtually the whole subject of unilateral monetary theory is unsound.

How can I be so dogmatic? I have extracted the facts and proved them by accounting examples.

The absence of a bibliography

A critic once said that I had scant regard for economists. This is not so. Each is a person of his or her own times, influenced by current views. My quarrel is with the teaching.

Nevertheless, if I am right, others must be wrong. As, however, I use different methods to arrive at my findings and my proof, I feel it is for me to state my case and not become involved in allocating blame for false theories.

I could, of course, try to give my views standing by sprinkling them with eminent names and prominent works. That, however, is not my way. I want my views to stand and prevail purely on their own merits.

That was also the case in respect of my other book, *The Monetary Analysis*, which is why it too does not contain a bibliography.

Challenging the Economic Establishment

Realising that the more I examined the transactions and settlements taking place in the economy, the further my findings were taking me from unilateral monetary theory, I sought to interest the economic establishment in them. I thought that this eminent body would welcome this different approach and be keen to discuss alternative concepts.

Apart from writing *The Monetary Analysis*, I sent papers to senior economists at various universities. Some did not reply, others simply repeated current arguments, which I was opposing, and one of the more helpful ones asked me what I sought to gain by sending papers to overworked and underpaid professors!

In addition, I corresponded with the Treasury and the Bank of England, with limited effect, and wrote letters frequently to the press. Some of these were published, but the subject matter is too large for these occasional successes to register to the extent needed.

Since it has become clear that I need to do more to have my views accepted by the economic establishment, I have devised an accounting formula for the basic money supply, showing its two-sided nature, with total service credits always equalling total service debts.

If I am correct, no transaction, event or abuse can put this formula out of balance. Thus, to prove that my version of monetary theory is unsound, all a challenger has to do is to find something to upset the formula, with all of economic history post-barter from which to choose!

This book, therefore, contains *inter alia* a solution to a mystery and a challenge. I trust that you, dear reader, will find the combination irresistible! That said, however, nothing should be allowed to detract from the seriousness of the issues raised, which are indeed of national importance.

Object

The object of this book is to replace unilateral monetary theory with the facts and not simply to contribute additional material. There is only room for one version – bilateral monetary theory.

1

The Trading System in Services

The bilateral definitions of money and money supply

We need to decide exactly what money is and to arrive at a precise definition.

In a primitive society, A performs a service, productive or otherwise, for B on the understanding that the latter will carry out a reciprocal one at a later date and accepts his IOU or simply his verbal promise. Money has been created; it is a credit in services of one party and a debt in services of another. A is a service creditor, B a service debtor. B redeems his promise by performing the reciprocal service and, if appropriate, recovers his IOU. Money has been destroyed. It is, therefore, subject to a process of continuous creation and destruction. Moreover, this basic situation is not altered by the use of third-party IOUs, such as banknotes.

As trade developed, many parties (individuals and groups) moved into credit in terms of services (service creditors), while the rest (service debtors) got into debt in services to the same extent. The transactions then became so intertwined that the credits and debts became respectively due from and to the community in general rather than to specific parties.

It became desirable to have evidence that the credits and debts existed, to measure them in common denominators and to have intervening devices, which would allow the values of the services to be exchanged at convenient times and in reasonable proportions.

In these circumstances, the economics profession defined money as anything which acts as a medium of exchange, a unit of account or a store of value. By so doing, they attributed the properties of the services to the measure, which is equivalent to defining therms as gas and logbooks as vehicles. In any case, a factor consisting of two separate sides cannot be represented adequately by a single item. Moreover, the definition makes no allowance for the true nature of the credits and debts and does not provide a collective term to describe them. It has made the rational discussion of 'money' somewhat difficult.

The profession should have realised that there are, in effect, two types of money: (1) basic money (credits and debts in services) and (2) nominal money (media of exchange and bank deposits). Nominal money is then a title to basic money in the same way as a deed is to a house. Basic money is the real kind, just as the house is the real property.

If wheat is measured by weight, it does not become something else, and neither do services when measured in a unit of account. The economics profession have, therefore, made a dreadful error in attributing the qualities of basic money to the nominal type.

The bilateral definition of basic money is, therefore, a credit in services of one party and a debt in services of another, measured in a unit of account – in our case, the pound.

It follows that the bilateral definition of the basic money supply is the total value of the service credits not yet spent, measured in the unit of account, or the total amount of the service debts not yet redeemed, also so measured. Total service credits always equal total service debts; in other words, savings always equal borrowings.

We also need a definition of nominal money. Thus, it is anything which acts as a medium of exchange or a unit of account. It is not, however, a store of value, as that is one of the qualities of basic money.

Consider this section with great care, for the recognition of basic as well as nominal money means that a new foundation and structure are necessary to replace currently accepted and falsely based unilateral monetary theory.

The foregoing example of A and B sets out the primitive situation, but the principle of the creation and destruction of basic money remains in force in present times. Thus, the modern economy works on the basis that all parties (individuals and groups) engaging in trading activities give their services in one capacity or another to the community and receive in return rights to buy the services of others.

Now, a modern B would not usually perform the reciprocal service directly for his counterpart, A. He would instead redeem his debt by performing services for other members of the community and A would spend his credit wherever he chose.

The origin and nature of basic money

The need for money, basic or nominal, does not arise when man gives his services without charge or engages in barter; it does, however, when one service has to be performed before another. Inevitably, therefore, the earliest money, which was basic and not nominal, was created by verbal promises to perform reciprocal services and existed whether or not it was evidenced in any way. Here is an example.

In a primitive society, a landowner asks a labourer to dig some ditches for him over a period of several weeks in return for food. The labourer cannot start until the following week, but the landowner agrees to commence the food supply from its beginning.

An obligation arises between them. It is bilateral – a credit in services of the landowner and a debt in services of the labourer, or, in other words, basic money.

At the end of each week, a credit will have been used up and a debt redeemed. Basic money is, therefore, subject to a process of continuous creation and destruction.

Suppose that the landowner does not trust the labourer. A mutual friend reassures him and undertakes to keep a weekly account of the transaction. The friend values a week's performance of both services at five units, credits this sum to the landowner and debits it to the labourer. Now, the friend is acting as a book-keeper and the transaction taking place *outside* the recording system is *reflecting* within it.

Alter the example. The friend arranges for the labourer to draw a cheque on him for five units; the labourer gives it to the landowner for the first week's food supply; and the landowner pays it into the 'bank'. Nothing has changed! The banker's figures are exactly the same as the book-keeper's! Basic money is *not*, therefore, created by bank lending.

Now let the loan be made in cash, printed by the banker, which follows the route taken by the cheque. Again, the same figures appear in the bank's books. Basic money is *not*, therefore, created by the printing press and the concept of 'a monetary phenomenon' is inevitably false.

It follows that the process by which basic money is created and destroyed relates to the trading system in services and takes place quite independently of any accounting procedure, banking system or note issue. This is a vitally important point.

There are two separate processes: (1) the trading activity and (2) the settlement systems. Basic money belongs to the former, nominal money to the latter. Bank lending is a later development of the settlement systems, the sole function of which is to facilitate trade.

The situation has been the same since primitive man first traded with his neighbour. Indeed, it cannot be changed, no matter how sophisticated our settlement procedures and systems become.

What do we use for payment?

Human beings, whether their work is productive or otherwise, trade solely in services. They always have and always will, for they have no other choice.

Look at any article you have purchased and ask yourself what you paid for it. No doubt you will name a price in cash terms, yet the correct answer is nothing. The raw materials, of which it is comprised, were supplied free by nature. What then did you pay for? The answer is the services of all the people, whose charges were included at the point of sale.

Consequently, it is just the services involved in production and supply which were paid for. The cost is recouped by a sale of goods, but the material element is always passed on without charge. Thus, it is not goods and services which are exchanged, but services alone.

In short, we pay nothing for goods; we pay only for services. Moreover, the concurrent creation of material wealth is simply a very valuable by-product of the system of trading in services!

What do we use for payment? People trade either as individuals or in groups, such as companies etc., and the term 'party' can be used to describe both capacities. Each party has either contributed more in services than obtained (service creditors) or the reverse is true (service debtors). Payments, therefore, reflect the alterations in the net positions of parties in terms of services. Thus, we pay in services. Creditor parties use up some of their credits in services; debtor parties increase their debts in services. Creditor recipients gain credits in services; debtor recipients reduce their debts in services.

Some services cannot be exchanged directly. Thus the landowner had to convert his services into a food supply before they could be exchanged. Goods, therefore, are the earliest form of a medium of exchange!

The continuous creation and destruction of basic money

Consider a further example of how basic money is created and destroyed.

In a primitive society, a farmer, whose crops have not yet ripened, seeks to buy a horse and offers in payment 100 sacks of wheat to be delivered shortly after harvesting has been completed. The seller agrees to this arrangement.

The creation of basic money is taking place. Since the farmer has no immediate means of making payment, he gets himself into debt instead. He becomes a service debtor. The horse-seller gains an asset, a credit of 100 sacks of wheat. He becomes a service creditor. Thus, in this case, basic money is the credit in services of the horse-seller and the debt in services of the farmer, measured in the unit of account, the sack of wheat.

As arranged, the farmer duly delivers the agreed quantity of wheat to the horse-seller. The reciprocal service has been performed, the debt repaid and the credit wiped out. Basic money has been destroyed.

The service creditor performed the first service (the delivery of the horse), while the service debtor carried out the reciprocal one (the delivery of the wheat). Thus, basic money is created when service creditors perform services for service debtors; it is destroyed when service debtors carry out reciprocal services for service creditors.

Even at this early stage, basic money supply credits are negotiable. The horse-seller could run up debts on undertaking to pass on some of the sacks of wheat. He would remain a service creditor, but to a lesser extent.

In the example, the service involved the provision of a horse. Basic money, however, would still have been created had the service taken any other form, productive or otherwise. The essential feature is that credits and debts in services arise. Total service credits always equal total service debts, whether the transactions in a community are taken separately or collectively. This principle still applies when credits have been negotiated and debts have been taken over.

There can be more than one party on either side of a transaction. Consequently, although total service credits always equal total service debts, the *number* of service creditors does not have to equal the *number* of service debtors.

Since basic money is created and destroyed by transactions, its quantity cannot influence the behaviour of the economy. Otherwise effect could influence cause.

Basic money is created and destroyed at the point where trade takes place and it can be observed that these events happen *outside* the banking system. Moreover, these principles apply even to the banks' own transactions as well as those they settle for their customers. Media of exchange, book-keeping and bank lending are simply developments in the settlement systems. They are means of improving the procedures and making more effective use of available resources. They have, however, no bearing on how basic money is created and destroyed.

The status rules

Some parties have given more value in services to others than have been reciprocated (service creditors), while, apart from the few occasionally in balance, the rest (service debtors) have, *to the same extent*, obtained more value in benefits than made in contributions. In addition, modern transactions are so intertwined that the credits and debts have, in effect, become respectively due from and to the community in general rather than to identifiable parties.

The two-sided nature of basic money shows up best in the double-entry book-keeping system used by British banks. Payments from borrowers to depositors show that basic money has been created and those in the opposite direction that it has been destroyed. The rest, between parties of like status, show that the constituent parts of the basic money supply have been altered, but that its total amount is unchanged. Remember, the changes take place outside the banking system and are reflecting within it.

Most transactions do not alter the statuses of parties, but in borderline cases they can easily so do. Indeed, leaving out the occasional situations when a party's status is neither service creditor nor service debtor, there can be nine different results on a before and after basis, as the following table shows:

Statuses Before		Statuses After	
Payer	*Recipient*	*Payer*	*Recipient*
Creditor	Creditor	Creditor	Creditor
Debtor	Debtor	Debtor	Debtor
Creditor	Creditor	Debtor	Creditor
Debtor	Debtor	Debtor	Creditor
Creditor	Debtor	Creditor	Debtor
Debtor	Creditor	Debtor	Creditor
Creditor	Debtor	Creditor	Creditor
Creditor	Debtor	Debtor	Debtor
Creditor	Debtor	Debtor	Creditor

A clear understanding of the effects on the basic money supply can be obtained by studying the next table. The principles involved are:

(1) Basic money supply is the total value of the service credits or the service debts, the answer being the same either way, or the part involved in a transaction.

(2) All transactions affect the constituent parts of the basic money supply.

(3) Payments from service debtors to service creditors show that the basic money supply has been increased.

(4) Payments from service creditors to service debtors show that the basic money supply has been reduced.

(5) Payments between parties of like status show that the basic money supply remains unchanged in total, but that its constituent parts have changed.

The balances of the parties have been provided for convenience and a payment of £150 is being made in each case.

Abbreviations used are: Cr (service creditor), Dr (service debtor), BMSD (basic money supply debts) and BMSC (basic money supply credits).

Statuses Before		Statuses After		BMSD	BMSC
Cr 200	Cr 200	Cr 50	Cr 350	–	–
Dr 200	Dr 200	Dr 350	Dr 50	–	–
Cr 100	Cr 100	Dr 50	Cr 250	+ 50	+ 50
Dr 100	Dr 100	Dr 250	Cr 50	+ 50	+ 50
Cr 200	Dr 200	Cr 50	Dr 50	–150	–150
Dr 100	Cr 100	Dr 250	Cr 250	+150	+150
Cr 200	Dr 100	Cr 50	Cr 50	–100	–100
Cr 100	Dr 200	Dr 50	Dr 50	–100	–100
Cr 100	Dr 100	Dr 50	Cr 50	– 50	– 50

Notes

(a) The effects on basic money supply credits and debts are always the same, as shown in the columns headed 'BMSD' and 'BMSC'.

(b) BMSD and BMSC are respectively the same as advances and deposits. This is not normally the case and only arises because of the limited nature of the illustration.

(c) On the third line, the first £100 is a payment from one service creditor to another, showing that basic money supply is unchanged in total, while the remaining £50 is from a service debtor to a service creditor, showing an increase to that extent.

(d) On the fourth line, the first £100 is a payment from one service debtor to another, showing that basic money supply is unchanged in total, while the remaining £50 is from a service debtor to a service creditor, showing an increase to that extent.

(e) The fifth line shows the main stream, which reduces the basic money supply. Most payments, in numbers and amounts, moving from service creditors to service debtors, are for purchases and in settlement of accounts.

(f) The sixth line shows the main stream, which increases the basic money supply. The main suppliers of goods and services are bank borrowers (service debtors) and transactions between them normally leave basic money supply unchanged in total. All, however, have to pay remuneration and the part going to service creditors causes a large increase in basic money supply.

(g) On the seventh line, the first £100 is a payment from a

service creditor to a service debtor, thereby showing that basic money has been reduced to that extent, while the remaining £50 is from one service creditor to another, leaving the total unaffected in its respect.

(h) On the eighth line, the first £100 is a payment from a service creditor to a service debtor, thereby showing that basic money supply has been reduced to that extent, while the remaining £50 is from one service debtor to another, leaving the total unaffected in its respect.

(i) On the ninth line, the first £100 is a payment from a service creditor to a service debtor, thereby showing that basic money has been reduced to that extent, while the remaining £50 is from a service debtor to a service creditor, showing an increase which results in a net reduction of £50.

It can be seen that for our purposes a payment which involves a change of status for one or both parties to a transaction has to be split at the point where each such change takes place. Three changes could be involved. For example, line nine could have read:

Before		*After*	
Cr 60	Dr 110	Dr 90	Cr 40

One can see at a glance that basic money supply falls by £20 when payment of £150 is made, but if the process is to be traced in full, three breaks are necessary. Thus, the payment can be treated as having been in instalments of £60, £50 and £40. The balances and statuses would change as follows:

	Balances		*Statuses*	
Starting position	Cr 60	Dr 110	Creditor	Debtor
Payment of £60	–	Dr 50	–	Debtor
Payment of £50	Dr 50	–	Debtor	–
Payment of £40	Dr 90	Cr 40	Debtor	Creditor

We can now see that, far from being a problem, the basic money supply is self-regulating and conforms to specific rules. For ease of reference, these can be described as 'the status rules'.

Who creates basic money? Who destroys basic money?

There are two parties to each transaction, so basic money and basic money supply can be considered from a unilateral point of view or from the joint stance. The situation from the *unilateral* point of view is as follows:

(a) Every service performed by a service creditor increases basic money supply credits (BMSC).

(b) Every service performed by a service debtor reduces basic money supply debts (BMSD).

(c) Spending by service debtors increases basic money supply debts (BMSD).

(d) Spending by service creditors reduces basic money supply credits (BMSC).

The actions of the service creditors bear on the credits, while those of the service debtors affect the debts.

In the previous section we considered nine possible combinations of statuses, but for practical purposes we need only deal with the four main ones, which are:

(a) A service creditor spending on services performed by another service creditor. (Creditor spending on creditor services.)

(b) A service debtor spending on services performed by another service debtor. (Debtor spending on debtor services.)

(c) A service debtor spending on services performed by a service creditor. (Debtor spending on creditor services.)

(d) A service creditor spending on services performed by a service debtor. (Creditor spending on debtor services.)

Basic money supply is made up jointly of credits (BMSC) and debts (BMSD) and each part of it is a credit in the hands of one party and the debt of another. Every transaction, therefore, alters the constituent parts of the basic money supply, but, nevertheless, BMSC always equals BMSD in total.

The effects on total basic money supply are as follows:

(a) Creditor spending on creditor services – no change. (The first party reduces basic money supply credits, but the second increases them to the same extent.)

(b) Debtor spending on debtor services – no change. (The first party increases basic money supply debts, but the second reduces them to the same extent.)

(c) Debtor spending on creditor services – an increase. (The first party increases basic money supply debts, while the second increases basic money supply credits to the same extent.)

(d) Creditor spending on debtor services – a reduction. (The first party reduces basic money supply credits, while the second reduces basic money supply debts to the same extent.)

Increasing basic money supply credits and increasing basic money supply are not the same thing. The first is a unilateral action, the second a joint one. Equally, there is a similar difference between reducing basic money supply credits and reducing basic money supply. Similar distinctions apply in the case of the debts.

Dubiety about the meaning of statements must be avoided. Consequently, in relation to the unilateral actions, reference will be made in the text to increasing or reducing basic money supply credits (BMSC) and basic money supply debts (BMSD), while the joint actions will be said to create or destroy basic money or basic money supply.

The joint position can now be summed up in a nutshell. Thus, basic money is created by debtor spending on creditor services and destroyed by creditor spending on debtor services. Moreover, these actions have similar effects on basic money supply.

Further comment falls to be made on the statement that there are two parties to each transaction. In practice, the party on one side or the parties on both sides could be made up of individuals and/or groups acting in concert. Their statuses need not be the same and, in such an event, the effect on basic money and basic money supply would be a net one. For example, if a service creditor and a service debtor acting together shared equally some spending on creditor services, the basic money supply would increase by half of the sum involved. This wider explanation should be borne in mind, but, for simplicity, reference will still be made to there being two parties to each transaction.

Basic money is created by debtor spending on creditor services. The debt is *in services*. Basic money is not, therefore, created by bank lending, as the debt involved is in terms of cash (nominal money) and does not involve the performance of services. For example, if Arthur borrows £100 from a bank, his net position is unaltered as he still has the cash and could give it back. His net position is, say, nil. If he spends the cash, he becomes a service debtor. When a service creditor buys goods from a service debtor, basic money is destroyed and again spending is the criterion.

We all engage in trade as individuals and often in concert with others. Thus, persons, trustees, firms, companies, commercial banks, the central bank, government departments and any other groupings are the participants in the market-place.

Commercial banks engage in two sets of operations, (a) those on behalf of their customers and (b) those on their own account. Customers' transactions take place outside the banking system and their effects on basic money supply occur at the point of spending. The banks simply carry out the settlement procedures and such actions do not affect the basic money supply. In regard to their own transactions, the situation is exactly the same and no different from that of any other participant in the market-place. Again, the transactions take place outside the banking system and the book-keeping records are amended to conform with what has happened.

Deposit-takers run their businesses on the same basis as any other company. Thus, they raise fixed capital from the public to buy assets and borrow their working capital from the banking system!

A bank balance sheet, stripped down to its essentials in relation to basic money, could in percentage terms read:

Deposits	100	Advances	92
		Cash	8
			100

What is not generally known is that Advances include an overdraft, granted by the bank to itself under a name such as 'The Bank's Account Current'.

It follows that since the banks are not behaving differently from other borrowers, (a) they cannot be creating basic money or (b) they are not the only ones so doing.

Which conclusion is correct? There are three main ways in which a bank can make a loan: (1) by granting an overdraft; (2) by crediting a customer's account and debiting a loan account in the same name; or (3) by issuing cash or a draft.

Nothing material has happened. The net positions of the customer and the bank are unchanged. In the first two cases the customer could cancel the facility and in the third return the cash or the draft.

Lending facilitates the creation of basic money, but is not the criterion. The loan has to be spent on creditor services. The second conclusion is, therefore, correct. Banks are not the only ones creating basic money.

Is the modern economy one in which (a) parties' claims on each other are still on a bilateral basis or (b) banks have been interposed, so that the claims are on them?

The notion that the banks have been interposed is false. Parties still trade freely amongst themselves and the resulting transactions are settled through the banking system *after* they have taken place. The additional features provided by the banks are, in the main, market-places for loans and safe places for deposits. Thus, the system was improved rather than materially altered.

In order to make a purchase or settle a debt, the payer has to offer (1) payment in kind or (2) a title to basic money supply credits (a medium of exchange) which is acceptable to the other party to the transaction. Thus, a personal IOU (a cheque) may be accepted. However, even if a cheque guarantee card is also required or payment in cash is demanded, neither a commercial bank nor the Bank of England becomes interposed. The obligation remains that of the payer and the effect in both cases is that the personal IOU then carries the guarantee of a third party. Accordingly, in the case of banknotes, it is just as if the Bank of England had written a guarantee on the payer's cheque.

Basic money was created by parties before banks came into

existence or governments took over the minting of coins or the printing of banknotes. This power has not disappeared. Accordingly, new practices do not alter the basic situation and simply facilitate the processes of settlement.

A borrower incurs two debts, one to the lender in cash and the other, on spending, to the community in services. The service debt has to be repaid by the performance of reciprocal services to obtain the funds to repay the loan. Thus, it is the service debt which affects the economy. Moreover, the loan can now be seen for what it really is – little more than an accounting device or borrowing from a friend.

Basic money is both a credit and a debt in services and as such is intangible. Methods of evidencing its existence and keeping account of it are, therefore, necessary. This principle applies to both the credits and the debts. For the purposes, media of exchange and book-keeping are required. Their use, however, does not alter the fact that it is services which are being exchanged.

In the early example, A performed a service for B without immediate payment. Put another way, B got the services of A on credit. Thus, any service debtor able to obtain goods and services on credit increases basic money supply debts, with the joint effects depending on the statuses of the other parties to the transactions.

B got the credit directly, but the principle applies equally when the credit is obtained via a third party, such as a bank or other deposit-taker. In these cases, however, basic money supply credits are needed to settle the purchase prices and come from depositors' funds. The lender parts with such credits and deposits become records of ownership instead of purchasing power. A creditworthy spender makes his purchases with borrowed basic money supply credits.

The suppliers of goods and services usually raise capital and obtain borrowing to finance their operations. These actions have no effect on basic money supply, but the subsequent spending on creditor services is the way in which new basic money is continuously created. Business and industry are main increasers and reducers of basic money supply debts.

Governments, too, are major service debtors. They increase basic money supply debts by spending and reduce them by levying taxes and charging fees.

Transactions involving the performance of services, such as work or the sale of goods, alter the constituent parts of the basic money supply, but those merely involving the movement of titles to basic money supply credits do not so do. Thus, depositing, withdrawing, lending or repaying have no effect on the quantity of basic money.

Since the quantity of basic money supply credits deposited is always adequate, banks have no need to create 'money' and simply lend their depositors' funds. Just as ownership of the deeds to a house allows the property to be let, so possession of the titles to the credits permits them to be lent.

Many rich parties are service debtors and run their affairs with the assistance of bank borrowing. Thus, material possessions make parties creditworthy and boost their ability to increase basic money supply debts.

Basic money is comprised of the personal service credits and the personal service debts of the parties creating it. Accordingly, no party's service credits or service debts are the same as those of any other party!

The same rules apply to all the participants in the market-place. Service creditors increase basic money supply credits (BMSC) by performing services and reduce them by spending; service debtors increase basic money supply debts (BMSD) by spending and reduce them with reciprocal services. In mundane terms, service creditors earn income and spend it, while service debtors spend themselves into debt and reduce their borrowings with earnings.

Every transaction alters the constituent parts of the basic money supply. The service credits can be negotiated and the service debts taken over. Nevertheless, total service credits always equal total service debts.

Who creates basic money? Parties in tandem engaging in transactions which result in debtor spending on creditor services.

Who destroys basic money? Parties in tandem engaging in transactions which result in creditor spending on debtor services.

Is basic money a 'flow' or a 'stock'?

Basic money is created, put to use and destroyed. Since creation must precede destruction, there is always an outstanding stock. It is, however, an ever-changing one, as the processes of creation, use and destruction are carried on.

The constituent parts of the basic money supply are in existence for varying lengths of time and differ in amounts. Consequently, a flow of basic money comes forward, serves purposes and is destroyed. Basic money is, therefore, more accurately described as a 'flow' than a 'stock'.

Goods have a similar existence. They are produced, bought and consumed. The outstanding stock is continually turned over – goods which are slow to move being sold at reduced prices. A continuous flow of basic money supply credits purchases goods from the stream of production and settles debts.

Nominal money has mistakenly been described as a stock. It represents basic money supply credits in use and has no independent existence from them.

Original and subsequent transactions

A distinction has to be made between original and subsequent (secondhand) transactions. The buyer of a new car pays for the services involved in its production and supply, but, if he sells it, the new owner does not so do. A subsequent sale is, therefore, a form of barter transaction, in which basic money is one of the items exchanged. The status rules still apply, as indeed they do to all transactions involving basic money. Thus, if a service creditor sells his car to a service debtor, basic money is created, while, if the statuses are reversed, it is destroyed.

Barter transactions only affect the parties concerned. Consequently, any gain to one party is at the expense of the other. It is of little importance, therefore, to the economy except as a reflection, if secondhand assets are increasing or decreasing in value. In regard, however, to original transactions, increases and decreases in the costs of the services involved alter the value of the unit of account and cause, respectively, inflation and deflation. Economic policies not directed at the cost of services are, as a result, ineffective.

Irredeemable service debts

Since basic money can be destroyed as well as created, it is important that both parts of the process should take place without major disruptions.

If the labourer in the example dies, any part of the service debt not completed becomes irredeemable and the landowner loses his service credit to the same extent. Thus, basic money can be destroyed by misfortune. In the same way, bankruptcies and liquidations result in the cancellation of service debts and an equal loss of service credits.

Continuous inflation regularly destroys part of the basic money supply, thereby preventing the economy from performing to its full capacity. Moreover, as is well documented, inflation can destroy a nation's savings. What has not been generally noted is that it also relieves the burden of borrowings to the same extent. Thus, the effects of the loss of service credits due to irredeemable service debts have not been fully appreciated.

The service credits and service debts are measured in the unit of account and the end result shows up as financial losses. Nevertheless, little importance has been attached to these as it is widely, but quite wrongly, assumed that one party's loss is another party's gain. In fact, major financial losses reduce the purchasing power in the community. Moreover, since trading activity is interlinked, the damage ripples through the economy with a domino effect. Most of the surviving businesses and industry are forced to contract and recession sets in. The process impoverishes part of the population.

In like vein, it is wrong to believe that the losses incurred by the survivors can simply be written off and have no effect on the economy. Losses in banking reduce the ability of the banks to lend, oblige them to raise interest rates, margins and fees, price the weaker creditworthy would-be borrowers out of the market and result in a lower level of trading activity being financed. Similarly, losses suffered by other organisations reduce their ability to trade.

Recessions, slumps and depressions can, therefore, be sparked off by losses in banking, insurance, property, industry, stocks and shares etc., when service debts become irredeemable and an equal quantity of service credits is destroyed.

There is then insufficient purchasing power in the economy to buy the current production of goods and services and the average standard of living has to fall. The greater the losses, the more severe will be the resulting contraction.

The effects are not felt evenly throughout the economy. This is because it contracts in an upward direction, causing more and more people to fall below the hardship line.

The economy reaches a point where it is viable again, but it is not catering adequately for the whole population. Worse still, there is no reason why it should automatically recover and, unless remedial action is taken to restore the lost working capital, a long period of stagnation, or even decline, can result. The corrective steps are a matter for later discussion.

Barter

The first trading system was barter – the direct exchange of goods and services – and resulted in immediate settlement. It is still in use to some extent today, but has largely been supplanted by subsequent developments. That, however, should not disguise the fact that from the very beginning, to present times, the primary purpose has been to exchange services.

Even when one type of goods is directly exchanged for another, it is the services making the trade possible which are being exchanged. Again, we note that goods were the first medium of exchange and are a by-product of the system of trading in services. The enormous value of the by-product should not conceal the fact that it is not an integral part of the trading system in services. Material wealth and financial wealth are two very different things.

When we are discussing the subsequent developments we must

keep in mind that the exchange of services is still the basis of the trading activity and the means by which basic money is created and destroyed.

Thus, no matter what media of exchange and bank deposits may appear to indicate, there can never be more basic money in existence than that owed by the service debtors to the service creditors.

2

The Settlement Systems

Media of Exchange

As already noted, nominal money is anything which acts as a medium of exchange or a unit of account. It is not, however, a store of value, for that is one of the qualities of basic money.

Communities which engage solely in barter do not need media of exchange. A point, however, is reached in human affairs, where people wish to be able to exchange their services for the things they need in the approximate quantities they want at convenient times. Basic money came into being and was first created by verbal promises. It should be noted, therefore, that basic money predates media of exchange.

Basic money is intangible. As trade expanded, it became necessary to have evidence of its existence and a means of transferring its ownership. Many things have been used for these purposes and among those frequently mentioned are cowrie shells, bags of salt, tobacco, silver and gold. In comparatively recent times, they have been replaced by forms of tokens, markers and IOUs, and the main ones in use today are cash and cheques. All such things, whether commodities, metals or vouchers, can be described as media of exchange.

A party intending to spend has a choice of using one of a variety of media of exchange for the proposed transaction. There is only one reservation: it must be acceptable to the intended recipient. Cash is a ready-made state medium of exchange and only needs one action to have a bearing on the basic money supply. That action is delivery. A cheque has first to be made out and then delivered. When a credit card is involved, the manifold form has to be completed, but again it is the handing over of the instruction part – delivery – which affects the basic money supply. Delivery is the point at which the trading of services between participants takes place.

Basic money is created, serves its purpose and is destroyed. Some of it is always outstanding and makes up the basic money supply. The overall process is one of creation and destruction and follows the same pattern as life itself. Media of exchange are caught up in this pattern and have no independent existence of their own. Thus, cheques are issued by drawers (creation), settle relevant transactions (purpose) and are debited to bank accounts (destruction). Cash, too, is similarly restricted. It is delivered (creation), settles relevant transactions (purpose) and is returned to the banking system (destruction).

Banknotes can be reissued, but we should not be deceived by this, as they move each time in a new set of circumstances unrelated to the previous ones. We have been led to believe that banknotes circulate from hand to hand all over the place in an unrestricted manner. In fact, they follow the same routes as cheques and serve the same purposes. In general, these routes are most often bank, drawer, shopkeeper and bank again. The life spans of banknotes and cheques are similar, but the former can enjoy more than one on reissue (reincarnation). A banknote moving in settlement of transactions is not 'working harder' and causing inflation.

The banks use the term 'dormant accounts' to refer to those on which no transactions have taken place for a considerable period of time. All accounts are, by the nature of things, dormant since the last transaction and a given period is not a suitable criterion for our purposes. We must regard 'deposited' as synonymous with 'dormant'.

Cash in wallets or purses has the same status as deposits. Thus, part of the total amount is virtually dormant, as the holders do not intend to release it, while the remainder is also in a static state for, although drawn to cover purchases and settle debts, it has not yet been put to those purposes. In the same way, shopkeepers will keep given amounts in their tills and have in mind that they will pay the excess into their bank accounts. When moving from a wallet to a till, cash goes from one dormant situation to another and settles a single transaction. On the same principle, a cheque transferred to a third party is settling two separate transactions.

Whoever owns bank deposits, or has access to them through a borrowing facility, can respectively reduce basic money supply credits or increase basic money supply debts by issuing a cheque. This instrument is normally credited to the payee's account; if it is a house cheque – one drawn on and paid in or cashed at the same bank branch – it will be debited on the day of receipt to the drawer's account; if not, it will be presented through the clearing system and allowed for in the settlement procedures; in either case, it will be cancelled by the drawee bank. Modern technology has removed the need for cheques to be physically presented, but the principles involved remain intact.

Banknotes and coin are, on issue by the authorities, deemed to be 'in circulation'. That is a misleading description as it gives the impression that they are active and busy. Media of exchange are neutral and have no wills of their own. They have to be pushed physically into use to settle transactions. 'Outstanding' is a more accurate description.

Cash can be drawn from a bank and placed in a wallet. At that stage, no change in status has taken place. Some funds being looked after by a banker have been converted to cash, but the depositor is no worse off. Equally, if the cash is part of a loan, the debtor's net position is unaltered. Movements of media of exchange not involving trading transactions do not usually affect the constituent parts of the basic money supply. Exceptions are gift and theft.

The delivery of a medium of exchange can cause different results, so it follows that such an item can never be basic money. Here is an example.

Allan washed the windows of the local bank branch, where he

maintains a creditor account. He was given a £20 note in settlement and paid it into his account. A service creditor (Allan) has performed a service for a service debtor (the bank). Basic money has been created and, in evidence, there is an increase in deposits and in the debtor balance of 'The Bank's Account Current'.

Two days later, Allan called at the branch to draw £20 and by chance was given the same note. He spent it on groceries. The grocer paid it into the branch, where he also has a creditor account. One service creditor (Allan) has reduced basic money supply credits by spending, while a second one (the grocer) has increased them to the same extent by performance of service. Total basic money supply is unchanged.

Allan called again at the branch and drew the same £20 note. This time he spent it on petrol at a nearby garage. The proprietor paid it into the branch in reduction of his overdraft. A service debtor (the proprietor) has performed a service for service creditor (Allan). Basic money has been destroyed and, in evidence, deposits and advances are down.

Thus, on the first occasion the passing of the note increased total basic money supply; on the second it left it unchanged in amount and on the third it reduced it. Clearly, the note cannot be basic (real) money. Again, we note that basic money is created and destroyed by the trading activity, while media of exchange assist in the settlement procedures.

In passing, I would mention that the 'The Bank's Account Current' is the control account, and expenditure would be debited to a subsidiary part of it named 'Charges Account'.

The amount of cash in circulation is determined by public demand. Thus, the government could issue notes and coin in settlement of purchases, but any part the public did not wish to keep would be returned via the banks. Transactions between the public and the government are settled at the close of business days and, unless they more or less break even, result in a surplus or a shortage in the money market, which requires action by the Bank of England. Thus, its usual practice is to sell Treasury Bills to the discount houses to mop up surpluses and to buy such securities from them to provide funds in cover of shortages. The excess cash would be dealt with under this procedure and the government would discover that it had been obliged to borrow all or part of the cost of its purchases.

The government, through its departments and agencies, is just as much a participant in the market-place as any other party. None of the participants can succeed with unilateral action, for, unless there is a coincidence of needs, a reaction, such as the returning of the unwanted cash, will take place. The government is a service debtor and spends in anticipation of its income. It can, therefore, increase basic money supply debts by spending and reduce them from its income. Thus, the principles are the same as for any other service debtor, though the scale of the transactions is much greater.

It has been contended that money (cash) is created by the Bank of England and must then be held. In fact, basic money can only be created by debtor spending on creditor services and obeys the status rules. Cash is nominal money.

The Bank of England issues banknotes for two reasons: (1) petty cash payments and (2) response to demand. Obviously, the first reason can be ignored, but, in regard to the second, it should be noted that the Bank demands, and has always demanded, immediate payment for every banknote it issues. Thus, banknotes are sold by the Bank and can only be purchased with – yes – real money! Service creditors buy them with basic money supply credits via the commercial banks or other intermediary; service debtors also buy them in this way, but the basic money supply credits they use for the purpose are borrowed. Again, we confirm that banknotes cannot be basic money. The Bank uses the purchasing power it receives to buy government securities, which it holds in cover of the note issue. Notes printed but not issued, and those returned to the Bank, are held in reserve. As such, they are completely inactive.

In truth, a banknote is simply a purchasing voucher for general purposes in the same way as a luncheon voucher is for a specific one. The position would be clear if banknotes bore a statement reading, 'This voucher is exchangeable for its face value in services'. The fact that banknotes are legal tender merely makes them more acceptable, but does not change their function in any other way.

No doubt the public will continue to describe media of exchange, such as cash, cheques, etc, as money, but if we are to solve our economic problems, there has to be an understanding of the true position, at least in academic, official and professional circles.

Deposits

We say loosely that money is deposited in banks. We must be more precise, for it is only the basic money supply credits that are paid in. Whatever the amount of these credits, there is a corresponding amount of debts elsewhere. It must be understood, therefore, that in respect of their customers' financial affairs, banks deal solely in basic money supply credits. This is a very important point and its implications have to be considered.

The introduction of media of exchange enabled basic money supply credits to be stolen. Thus, whoever gained possession of a bearer medium of exchange acquired the rights to services it represented. A need arose for safe places to keep the credits. In this country, it was originally met by the strongboxes of the goldsmiths and in present times is accommodated by the vaults of the banks. Banking systems came into existence and have been developed.

Media of exchange can be used for moving basic money supply credits without altering their ownership, such as by deposit, withdrawal, lending or repayment. In these cases, the credits are transferred to the recipients, who are enabled to make use of them.

Banks utilise all the basic money supply credits which come into their hands for one purpose or another and retain only about eight per cent in cash. While, therefore, banks were originally formed to keep the credits in safe custody, they developed into organisations which put them to use.

A ledger account shows the entries which have been posted through it. The balance of the account is the amount of basic money supply credits due to or by the customer. The systems of trading and banking work, both here and abroad, because communities have agreed by common consent to honour the depositors' rights of ownership and service debtors are normally ready to redeem their obligations by performing reciprocal services.

Nowadays most service creditors deposit their surplus funds with banks and building societies, and facilities to draw cheques may be available from both types of organisation. Large parts of the balances are not needed for routine transactions and are clearly dormant. In fact, that is the nature of all deposits. The basic money supply credits are not needed immediately and are put into the custody of the recipients. They can, however, be reactivated by the drawing of cheques.

Deposits are basic money supply credits at the times they are placed with the custodians. How then can they lose this status? The recipients lend their customers' credits, but do not reduce deposits. That omission changes the nature of deposits. Thus, instead of being evidence of purchasing power held by the custodians on behalf of their creditor customers, they change to records of to whom those recipients owe basic money supply credits, most of which are no longer in their possession. The deposit-takers maintain their records in the way which suits them best, but one result is the wide misunderstanding of the nature of deposits.

Differences between deposits and basic money

As already noted, deposits are records and make no allowance for the fact that the recipients use their customers' funds to finance lending. Thus, with a single entry book-keeping system, advances would be deducted correctly from deposits. As things are, however, there are many differences between deposits and basic money.

Kenneth is a service debtor; he has a creditor bank account and a large loan from a building society. Laurie is a service creditor and has a creditor bank account. Spending by Laurie on Kenneth's services would reduce basic money supply and yet result in payment from one depositor to another; spending by Kenneth on Laurie's services would increase basic money supply and again leave deposits unchanged in amount. Thus, basic money supply can rise and fall while deposits remain unchanged in amount.

Martin is a service debtor and has a bank overdraft. Spending by Kenneth on Martin's services would leave basic money unchanged in amount, but deposits and advances would both fall; spending by

Martin on Kenneth's services would leave basic money unchanged in amount, yet deposits and advances would both rise. Thus, basic money can remain unchanged in amount while deposits rise and fall.

Debtor spending on creditor services, nevertheless, normally reflects in an increase in deposits. The economics profession have seized upon this process and mistakenly attributed the cause to bank lending. Moreover, they believe that it results in a build-up of deposits, which they regard as competing purchasing power and a cause of inflation. The fact that the other process, by which basic money is destroyed, is going on at the same time is ignored. Indeed, they seem to be blissfully unaware that it exists. There is, therefore, no justification on any grounds for believing that the build-up of deposits is due to bank lending.

What then causes the build-up? Under barter, trade and settlement are simultaneous, but nowadays there is a widening gap between them. The massive supply of goods and services is financed by bank lending and we are not usually asked to make stage payments for work in progress. In addition, many services have already been provided, but the bills, such as for electricity, have not yet been presented. Accordingly, deposits are allowed to build up.

The build-up does not stop with the settlement procedures. Accounting systems can cause a proliferation of deposits, which are clearly not purchasing power. Banks, for example, maintain creditor accounts with the Bank of England, designated 'Bankers' Deposits', the contras of which are debtor accounts in their own books; thus, the balances at the central bank are double-counted. Indeed, this situation happens when any deposit-taker has a creditor account with another.

Actually, the position could be worse as banks calculate the netted positions of some customers. This means that they set off the debtor and creditor balances in their books of the same parties and arrive at a net answer for each one. Total deposits and total advances can then be reduced by the total amount set off. As a result, the total netted balances of deposits and advances in any bank are much lower than the ledger (or computer) ones.

Many corporate customers, however, maintain a mixture of debtor and creditor accounts with more than one bank and often at several branches of a bank. Under present circumstances, complete netting of all balances is not, therefore, possible.

Like Kenneth, many customers of building societies have loan and deposit accounts in the same name, which can only be set off if they are with the same organisation. Moreover, by the nature of the way we live, practically all parties have income due and outstanding debts; thus, they are net service creditors or net service debtors. A service creditor makes a purchase from a service debtor using his credit card. Creditor spending on debtor services has reduced the basic money supply. The purchaser now has a creditor account with his bank and a debtor one with the credit card company. The position will be rectified when he issues his cheque in payment of the debt, but it should be noted that the settlement procedures lag behind the process of the creation and destruction of basic money. The net position is the real one.

Banks accept deposits in the principal foreign currencies as well as in sterling and keep a record of ownership in their books. The funds, however, are redeposited with their branches or correspondent banks in the relevant foreign countries. Such currency appears as deposits in the books abroad, while the sterling values can be included in the figures for deposits of the British banks. For our purposes, basic money supply credits should not appear in two sets of books.

For all these reasons, deposits are very far from being purchasing power and their real function is simply to serve as bank records. Purchasing power is actually the part of deposits savers intend to spend plus the part borrowers have obtained for the same purpose.

Too much attention has been given to the book-keeping figures of the banks while the processes of the creation and destruction of basic money have been overlooked. We must no longer allow ourselves to be deceived by the records of the banks. These records suit the banks, but cannot reflect correct answers for total basic money supply measured either in service credits or service debts.

The mistaken beliefs that deposits are purchasing power and that banks create money by lending are widely held owing to the false teaching. Those deposits greatly exceed the basic money supply credits held by the banks and a question arises as to how the excess should be described. For example, gross deposits and net deposits would give undeserved standing to the former, when the difference between the two consists purely of cross entries, some internal and some between deposit-takers. Thus, it represents nothing; perhaps 'froth' would suffice. Realise that, if the froth were real purchasing power, there would have to be a corresponding amount in basic money supply debts. The mind boggles!

Another point to consider is, of course, inflation; it results in deposits being represented by more and more pounds of less and less value.

No book-keeping system can alter the facts; it can only reflect or misrepresent them.

Borrowing

The issues in this section were discussed in my book, *The Monetary Analysis*, under the heading, 'The Theory of the Recirculation of Money'. Since, however, basic money does not circulate and can only be used once, this heading is inappropriate. The process involved is correctly described, but it is media of exchange which pass from hand to hand and give the impression that basic money is circulating.

A monetary system is a natural development in human affairs and appears to have been introduced in many separate places. It was accepted by general consensus and is now operated on an international scale. The consensus created a set of rules.

Because basic money is subject to destruction, it has to be generated on a continuous basis by trading activity. Moreover, the level of that activity determines the standard of living. For these reasons, there has to be enough purchasing power in the community to enable its transactions to take place, and an adequate supply of nominal money.

Saving, as such, has no merit. Indeed, it can be seen that by not spending savers slow down the system and prevent other members of the community from performing reciprocal services.

The drawback is that, owing to differences in ability, luck, character, etc, basic money supply credits accumulate in the hands of some parties. This deprives other parties of access to the credits and obliges them to work for, or borrow from, the savers.

The practice of borrowing is, therefore, a great advance, enabling as it does a vast increase in trading activity and a corresponding rise in the standard of living.

The need to borrow is particularly felt by the producers of goods, who have to sustain themselves, their families, their industries and their employees during the period of production. Before the banks came on the scene, the producers had to borrow from the parties in whose hands basic money supply credits were accumulating. Thus, the monetary system created the pressure to borrow.

When the banks arrived, the accumulating funds were deposited with them and would-be borrowers were forced to apply for advances. The banks were happy to take over the lending function in return for repayment plus interest.

The following points can be noted:

(a) The deposit of cash with the banks by service creditors has the effect of placing basic money supply credits out of reach in safe custody.

(b) Purchasing power in the community is then insufficient to enable all the transactions necessary to maintain the standard of living to take place.

(c) The situation is relieved by bank lending, which allows the process of the creation of basic money to be resumed when the borrowers spend themselves into debt on creditor services.

(d) Banks, by lending, assist the process, but are not the catalysts.

It is not necessary for every transaction to be settled by cash, and the use of cheques for the purpose became popular. Nevertheless, the number of transactions taking place in the community is governed by the level of trading activity and the new means of settlement does not increase that number, except to the extent that the very convenience of the method makes a higher level of trading activity possible. In many cases, cheques replaced cash and became media of exchange. Thus, they represent basic money supply credits during the course of their use, just as cash performing the same function does. A banknote and a cheque are simply two pieces of paper with an equal ability to act as a medium of exchange to the extent of their face values and their acceptability.

Cash replaced by cheques is paid by the banks into their accounts with the Bank of England. Nothing of consequence is changing, for the deposits of cheques with the banks by service creditors has exactly the same effects as the deposit of cash.

Banks are, therefore, able to make their profits by lending their depositors' funds and have no need to 'create credit, and hence money, by lending', even if they could. Equally, cash in their tills is not needed as a base for the mythical pyramid of credit. It must be remembered, however, that borrowing is not a one-way flow, for the performance of reciprocal services by service debtors is continuing to destroy basic money and shows up in a movement of funds from deposits to advances.

Basic money, as we have observed, does not circulate, and the process by which the credits accumulate in the hands of certain parties carries on. This, in turn, provides more funds to the banks in the form of deposits and forces more borrowing. Thus, deposits and advances grow. In practice, they can grow until all the surplus funds have been deposited and the main borrowing requirements of the service debtors are being met. They reflect the level of trading activity and to that extent their growth is healthy.

Companies and firms reach the stage where they are profitable, although they continue to borrow for working capital purposes. In turn, this should produce a certain stability in the growth of deposits and advances, but the picture is being obscured by inflation. Nevertheless, the growth of deposits and advances through trading activity is healthy and their growth from inflation is a reflection of troubles outside the control of the banking system.

In Britain, we have a very efficient banking system. It automatically transfers the surplus funds to London and makes the City the main centre for major loans. Even the residue is put to use by being lent overnight to the money market.

Borrowing cannot exceed the available deposits and increases in demand for it are curbed by rising interest rates. Alternatively, low demand allows interest rates to fall.

The weakness, which is not of the system, lies in the uses to which the borrowing is put. These, we shall discover, are far too important to be left simply to the market forces.

Lending

We have already noted that a borrower incurs two debts, one to the lender in terms of cash and the other, on spending, to the community in terms of services. Lending, as well as borrowing, has other facets, so the two practices are not simply each other's counterpart. We must know what is being lent.

The economy could possibly work to a reasonable extent without lending, if we all spent our incomes upon receipt on purchases and advance payments. That, however, is not the situation, so lending is necessary to make use of the dormant deposits. It is an additional and separate practice, which finances the supply of goods and services and allows some parties to live beyond their immediate means. In so doing, it gives a boost to the standard of living.

Lending has to be financed. Moreover, neither a bank nor any other party can lend something not in their possession. Thus, the banks, having no funds of their own, use the dormant deposits for the purpose.

How do we describe this practice? To say that the banks are 'recirculating money' contradicts the facts that basic money does not circulate and can only be used once. That statement, however, refers to the process by which basic money is created and destroyed, and not to the practice of lending.

A bank making a loan in cash hands over depositors' basic money supply credits; the borrower uses them for expenditure; the recipients pay them into their bank accounts, creditor or debtor; and the depositors' funds are thus returned to the banking system, with each bank more or less recovering its market share.

The bank may instead grant an overdraft facility; the borrower issues cheques for expenditure; the cheques are met on presentation with depositors' basic money supply credits and are settled through the clearing system; and again each bank more or less recovers its market share.

Lending is carried out on a continuous basis and on a vast scale, so the depositors' funds outside the banking system amount to a massive sum. Thus, advances in total represent the extent to which depositors' basic money supply credits are in use for lending purposes. Some deposits are being spent and fresh ones keep coming in. It is not a case, therefore, of all the same funds being in continuous use.

None of this interferes with the increases and reductions in basic money supply debts, when borrowers respectively engage in spending or perform reciprocal services. The net effects, of course, depend on the statuses of the other parties to the transactions. As usual, the status rules apply.

It would seem best to say that banks 'use their depositors' funds to finance lending'. There is no 'creation of money' in this action. Payment can only be made with basic money supply credits, whether they are owned or borrowed.

The important issue is that we should understand what is happening. This is particularly so when it is being taught mistakenly that 'banks create credit, and hence money, by lending'. Here is an example in support of the contention and the reasons why it should be rejected.

Customers of a goldsmith deposit gold to the value of £5,000; he lends 10 per cent to a merchant. His books show:

Liabilities		Assets	
Deposits	£5,000	Gold	£4,500
		Loan	500
			£5,000

Prior to this transaction, deposits and gold were both £5,000. Consequently, it is contended that, while no increase has taken place in the goldsmith's liabilities, £500 of gold has gone into circulation. The merchant uses the gold to buy goods from a manufacturer and the latter redeposits it with the goldsmith, making the balance sheet read as follows:

Liabilities		Assets	
Deposits	£5,500	Gold	£5,000
		Loan	500
			£5,500

The deposits, which can theoretically be turned into gold on demand, now exceed the quantity of the metal held. In fact, of course, the deposits can only be turned into gold if the loan is repaid. The interpretation of the balance sheet is wrong. Deposits are simply the goldsmith's record of what he owes, just as the loan shows the amount due to him. Separate gold into 'received' and 'delivered' and examine the resulting balance sheet.

Liabilities		Assets	
In ⟶ Deposits	£5,500	→ Gold received	£5,500 ⌐
Out ← Gold delivered	500	← Loan	500 ↵
	£6,000		£6,000

Now, by following the arrows, it can be seen that gold simply flows through the hands of the goldsmith. There is no creation of anything in this action. He could keep his stock in such a way that gold received was stacked at the back, while that delivered was taken from the front. Thus, the theoretical idea of a flow of gold becomes fact.

When the loan was made, the contention was that while no increase had taken place in the goldsmith's liabilities, £500 of gold had gone 'into circulation'. Since £5,000 of gold came out of circulation, how can the goldsmith reasonably be accused of starting a process of 'money creation' by releasing a mere 10 per cent of it?

Reconsider the example knowing that the process of the creation and destruction of basic money, on the one hand, and the practice of lending, on the other, are separate issues. It can be seen that the increase in deposits from £5,000 to £5,500 is a correct reflection of the basic money created by the debtor spending of the merchant on the creditor services of the manufacturer.

In regard to the gold, media of exchange (and bank records) are needed to evidence the existence of basic money and to transfer its ownership (gift or theft) or possession (deposit or loan). They have no separate existence of their own and are used for specific purposes. Thus, £5,000 of basic money supply credits were deposited with the goldsmith, though a further weakness of the example is that it does not show who owes the corresponding basic money supply debts.

The goldsmith transferred £500 of depositors' funds to the merchant; he used them for his purchases; and the manufacturer returned them to the goldsmith.

We have to recognise that a bank, in the first place, acts as a custodian of purchasing power by taking deposits and, in the second, borrows most of that purchasing power. It onlends most of these funds and uses the rest for its own purposes!

Each bank can borrow all the purchasing power deposited with it (BMSC) and that is exactly what it does, with the exception of its holding of cash. Building societies and other deposit-takers behave in the same way. In respect of a bank, here are some examples:

(a) Advances. It borrows depositors' funds and lends them.

(b) Working Capital. It borrows depositors' funds to cover the overdrawn balances of 'The Bank's Account Current'.

(c) Investments. It borrows depositors' funds and buys investments in its own name.

(d) Bank of England Account. It borrows depositors' funds and places them in an account in its own name with the Bank of England.

(e) Cross Entries. It borrows depositors' funds and pays them into creditor accounts in customers' names; thus, in effect, it takes the funds out as a borrower and places them afresh with itself as a custodian! The purpose is normally to lend the funds to the customers, so the credits will not remain for long.

(f) Money at Call. It borrows depositors' funds and lends them to the discount houses.

(g) Fixed Assets. If its fixed assets exceed its capital, it has borrowed depositors' funds to cover the difference.

We have noted that the deposit of funds by some parties forces others to come to the banks for their borrowing requirements. Moreover, it has been shown that the community needs most of its basic money supply credits to be used to finance lending in order to maintain the level of trading activity and the standard of living. It is important, therefore, that basic money supply credits should pass through the hands of the banks rather than remain with them.

Gold, as we saw, could be treated by a goldsmith in this way and his books could be kept to show what was happening. Moreover, it would have made no difference if he had issued gold certificates instead of gold, except for the fact that the convenience of such a method might have permitted more transactions to take place.

Now we can concoct an extract from a bank's books and treat the figures in the same way.

£ million			*£ million*	
In ⟶ Deposits	£100	⟶ Funds received	£100	
		⌐ Advances	← 50	←
Out ← Funds delivered	70 ←⌐ Investments	← 20	
	£170		£170	

With the routes established, basic money supply credits can flow through the hands of the bank. They have to be pushed every step of the way. The extract has been simplified, but the addition of all the other items in a bank's balance sheet would not affect the principle. Banks borrow all their deposits except the cash holding and put them to use one way or another. When the demand for one item rises, another falls. Thus, in the example, advances rise and fall conversely with investments. The relationship is clearly established and the notion of a build-up of 'credit and money' disappears. Basic money supply credits flow into the hands of parties as income and borrowing and back out again as expenditure and loans. All the participants in the market-place have this experience and the banks are no exception. The monetary system is much more stable than it has been given credit for!

In the example, the merchant's debtor spending on the manufacturer's creditor services caused an increase in basic money supply. If the manufacturer had been a service debtor, the spending would have resulted instead in old debt of his being replaced by new debt of the merchant. It can be seen, therefore, that every loan does not create a deposit and that a very large part of trading activity takes place between service debtors.

Notice how the media of exchange are tied to the trading activity. Cash and cheques follow the same routes as the gold. There is no question of 'money sloshing around'.

Perhaps the banks, instead of lending, should invite depositors and borrowers to auctions, where the loans would go directly to the highest bidders. The banks could charge a fee for each loan agreed and would incur neither the risks of lending nor the expense of taking security. This system would not be so efficient, but it would be a dramatic way of ridding ourselves of the notion that banks create money by lending.

It may look an extreme and far-fetched solution. Nevertheless, it is interesting to note that banks have taken some modest steps in that direction. Thus, some major loans have been securitised. This means that they have been grouped together and sold as company debt in much the same way as is the government kind.

Redispositions

A transaction involving the transfer of basic money supply credits without services for value being rendered requires a name, and I have chosen 'redisposition'. Many of the movements of cash and other media of exchange come under this classification. Depositing, withdrawing, lending and repaying are obvious examples, as they do not change the statuses of the parties involved.

It has been said that 'all modern money is the liability of financial organisations'. That would mean that cash is basic, rather than nominal, money. In considering redispositions, we can correct this misconception.

In Britain, cash consists of notes issued by the Bank of England, the note issue of the Scottish banks to the extent it is uncovered, and coin emanating from the Royal Mint.

The Bank of England can issue notes for three reasons:

(a) In response to withdrawals by depositors;

(b) as loans to borrowers;

(c) by spending.

(a) Its Banking Department carries on a normal banking business, but its customers are mainly government departments and commercial banks. It could be called upon to provide cash directly for, say, wages for the armed forces or nationalised industries, but arrangements are usually made for cash to be drawn from local branches of the commercial banks against presentation of cheques or under credits. The main outflows, and for that matter inflows, are therefore through the commercial banks in response to variations in public demand.

When cash is withdrawn, 'Deposits' fall and 'Notes in Circulation' rise. The Banking Department transfers some of the government securities it holds to the Issue Department as cover for the increase. This process is reversed when cash flows back to the Bank of England due to falling public demand, but inflation ensures that the trend is to an ever-increasing note issue.

In responding to withdrawals, the Bank of England does not incur an additional obligation and consequently there is no change in the basic money supply; similarly, the commercial banks are withdrawing cash for their own purposes and not performing services for monetary reward. Basic money supply credits are being moved by the medium of exchange, but ownership is not being transferred. The custodian is returning the owner's property. Equally, there is no effect on basic money supply when cash flows from the commercial banks to the Bank of England.

(b) In making loans to government departments, the Bank of England meets their cheques. Moreover, it does not generally allow private customers to have accounts, though it has in some exceptional cases. It has little reason, therefore, to issue notes on a scale of any consequence directly to borrowing customers. When, however, it does issue notes to borrowers, the effect on the assets of the

Banking Department is that cash falls and advances rise. Basic money supply credits have not been paid out in return for the performance of services. Equally, there is no obligation on the borrower to perform reciprocal services, though there is a duty to repay. As usual, lending does not increase the basic money supply.

(c) In all probability, the Bank of England does not use much cash for its own spending. Every organisation, however, needs to make some petty cash payments. These are in return for the performances of services and, since the Bank is a service debtor, increase basic money supply debts. It has, of course, a large amount of continuous expenditure which it settles in other ways, and that has a much greater effect on the basic money supply.

As noted, the main outflow of cash is to the commercial banks. We can now examine the three reasons why they pay out notes to the public, which are:

(a) In response to withdrawals by depositors;

(b) as loans to borrowers;

(c) by spending.

(a) When cash is withdrawn from a creditor account, the custodian is returning the owner's property. The customer, a service creditor, does not perform services in return for the cash, so the basic money supply is unchanged. Basic money supply credits are being moved by the medium of exchange, but ownership is not being transferred. Assets of the bank (cash) and liabilities (deposits) both fall.

(b) When a borrower withdraws cash from a bank, nothing is changed except the representation of the indebtedness. The net debtor position is the same. As always, a service debtor increases basic money supply debts by spending and reduces them by performance of services. Neither of these actions has taken place. Lending does not increase the basic money supply.

(c) Commercial banks, too, do not use much cash for their own spending. Small branches do employ some direct labour, such as cleaners, and have wages to pay in cash. These and other petty cash payments are in return for the performance of services and, as the banks are service debtors, alter the basic money supply in accordance with the status rules.

When cash is paid into a bank, it increases deposits, reduces advances or does both in part. It will now be readily understood that this action has no effect on the basic money supply. The action which increased that supply, reduced it or left it unchanged in amount, occurred when the transaction, for which the customer acquired the cash, took place. The media of exchange have served their purpose, having been, in effect, deactivated and returned to base.

The banking system consists of the Bank of England, commercial banks, building societies and the other licensed deposit-takers. The organisations comprising it are participants in the market-place, just like any other group or individual. Trading transactions on their own accounts, whether between themselves or others, take place outside the banking system and are recorded within it. They conform to the status rules. My collective name for the group is the 'Pool'.

In contrast, movements of cash within, and changes to the records of, the banking system, amounting only to redispositions, have no bearing on the basic money supply. They can be easily identified as the recipients are not being paid for the performance of services.

Basic money has not changed in character down through history. All modern versions of it are still the liabilities of the service debtors, who increase basic money supply debts by spending and reduce them from earnings. These debts are subject to redisposition when taken over.

Rotating cash reserves

In the discussion on the goldsmith, we noted how gold flowed through his hands when he arranged his holdings, so that the latest deposits were placed at the back, while loans were made by removing the required amounts from the front. Here are two transactions:

(1) A service debtor borrows a quantity of gold from a goldsmith and spends it on creditor services; the recipient deposits it in a creditor account with the goldsmith.

(2) A service creditor withdraws a quantity of gold from the goldsmith and spends it on debtor services; the recipient uses the gold to reduce his indebtedness to the goldsmith.

In both cases, the medium of exchange (gold) circulates and returns to the goldsmith, but the first transaction increases the basic money supply, while the second reduces it. The goldsmith acts as the banking system and movements to and from it do not affect basic money supply. It can be seen that transactions are independent of one another and that, unlike media of exchange, basic money is not circulating; it is being created and destroyed.

Every transaction of the goldsmith involves the receipt or delivery of gold and his stock of it is adequate for his business. If he changes over to issuing gold certificates, they will perform the same function as the gold, but will not in themselves increase his business. They will, however, be a more convenient method of settlement and the saving of time, coupled with the achievement of greater efficiency, may permit more trade to take place. The goldsmith could then be called upon to provide more facilities. Both the outward and inward flows would then increase, so the stock of gold could remain adequate. There is nothing inflationary in this situation, as trade and basic money supply are growing in step, provided that prices are not being raised.

The equivalent of the goldsmith's stock of gold in a modern commercial bank is a reserve consisting of the holding of cash, the balance of its account with the Bank of England and money at call with the discount houses. It also holds some readily realisable government stocks, but would only have to resort to them in very rare circumstances. The business of the bank is based upon this reserve. It is usually adequate to fund all transactions, because the main service debtors, corporate customers, have arranged facilities to finance the supply of goods and services, the bulk of which will be sold to the depositors. Thus, an increase in trade, soundly financed, could merely result in increased receipts and payments. A bank's business rises and falls in step with the trade it finances.

When banks operate a branch system, notes and coin are held in many places and are turned over on the same principle as any other reserve. The correct image is, therefore, of an ever-changing rotating reserve.

The businesses of building societies are also based upon similar reserves. Thus, building societies also use their depositors' funds to finance their lending.

Since all trade can be conveniently financed by the rotating reserves, there is no place for the additional 'money', which is wrongly supposed to be created by bank lending. It has been contended that 'banks can create money to the extent of $12^1/_2$ times their cash reserves'. Had this been true, a massive distortion would have taken place in our financial affairs and inflation would be running at very high rates, particularly as there is no way trade could have multiplied in step. In the event, there is some distortion, but it comes from outside the monetary system and is the result of the dilution of the currency caused by people obtaining more and more debased units of basic money for their services. The total amount of basic money outstanding at any one time is the value of the credits in services not yet spent and the contra debts unredeemed. The supply can be revalued in cash terms by practices which alter the purchasing power of the unit of account, but in service terms it cannot be changed except by rises and falls in the trading activity.

Media of exchange circulate. In the normal course, as noted, they leave the banking system, settle a transaction and return to base. Payment by cheque short-circuits the full procedure, but the effect is the same. One could claim that the circuits are started when the chequebooks are issued. On that basis, cheques complete the full course. The customer has a choice of using cash or a cheque for settlement purposes. Thus, these two types of media of exchange perform the same function. Accordingly, cash follows the same routes as cheques and returns regularly to the banking system. It does not pass endlessly from hand to hand outside the banking system, so when we say that it circulates and rotates, the limitations on its behaviour must be fully appreciated.

The flows of funds

Continuous borrowing and repayment are necessary to finance the production of goods and the provision of services, because we are not usually required to make advance or stage payments. In consequence, we can only buy immediately the available goods and services. As we do so, a constant, but not necessarily even, flow of funds moves into the debtor accounts of the suppliers. This is the general picture, as a proportion of the suppliers will be operating with creditor accounts and some purchasers will be using borrowing facilities. Moreover, many of the participants, whether individuals or groups, will frequently change from service creditors to service debtors and vice versa. A seething amount of activity and changing of places is going on, but the basic pattern remains constant. The main borrowers are always producers of goods or providers of services and are corporate customers.

Personal customers usually borrow to finance the purchase of goods and/or services, examples being a house, a car, a refrigerator or fees. The proceeds of the loans pass into the accounts of the suppliers, thus helping to keep down corporate indebtedness. New borrowing replaces old. Repayment of personal borrowing is usually made in monthly instalments and is expected to come from future income.

Funds flow down regular channels and our concern is with the main ones. In respect of corporate borrowing, the stages are as follows:

(a) A facility (short term fixture, term loan or overdraft) is agreed, which enables the customer to draw or utilise deposited funds by issuing cheques. In other words, the lender uses the dormant deposits to meet the cheques on presentation.

(b) The funds are utilised to purchase raw materials, pay wages and salaries, meet other expenses, etc.

(c) Goods and services are sold to depositors.

(d) Deposited funds flow into the borrowers' accounts, wiping out indebtedness in the order in which it was taken. The debtor balance of an account is always made up of the last cheques posted.

The funds are going round in a circle. They flow into the hands of the deposit-takers as deposits and repayments and out as withdrawals and loans. The outgoing funds never catch up with the incoming, so there is always a holding of cash, the rotating reserve.

Incidentally, it can be noted that the ratio of the reserve to deposits is largely irrelevant.

An illustration of the way in which the funds are circulated may help.

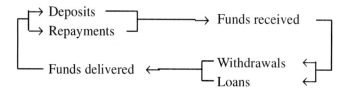

Basic money supply credits can be negotiated and transferred, but the debts can only be taken over. One result is that the deposit-takers deal solely in the credits or, in other words, in only one side of the basic money supply.

The circulation of the credits, therefore, facilitates the process by which basic money is created and destroyed. Some of the credits are being withdrawn for spending by service creditors and the rest by service debtors. The effects on the basic money supply, in accordance with the status rules, are very real; they are, however, not particularly visible, except to the extent to which the levels of deposits are being affected in real terms as opposed to inflationary ones. It makes no difference whether cash, cheques or any other media of exchange are used to circulate the credits.

The settlement process is already in operation. Consequently, whenever we look at the situation, deposits already include a proportion intended to cover debts being incurred and proposed purchases or, in a nutshell, commitments. Deposits do not simply grow. They rise and fall in accordance with the level of trading activity being financed by borrowing. Thus, an increase in the spending of borrowed funds would push up deposits, while a decrease would reduce them. That, of course, is a net effect, as many transactions are between parties of like status.

It is now clear that society has a recurring need. The cost of the production of goods and the provision of services has to be financed up to the point of sale and one big revolving bridging loan is the answer. This, in effect, is what the lenders are providing, regardless of how the facilities are provided. New 'money' from the banks is not required; all that is necessary is a means of access to the dormant deposits.

In respect of personal borrowing the stages are:

(a) The facility is agreed.

(b) The relevant sum is debited to an account in the customer's name and credited to his or her current account.

(c) The funds are utilised and the credit disappears.

(d) Goods are purchased and the borrowing of the suppliers is reduced.

(e) Personal borrowing has replaced corporate finance.

(f) The debt due to the lender will be repaid in instalments from future income.

Building societies attract considerable sums from the public in the form of deposits and use the funds to provide loans for house purchase transactions. They pay the funds received into their bank accounts and issue cheques for settlement purposes. The buyers grant mortgages to the societies in security and effect repayment in monthly instalments over periods of years.

Nowadays, the banks grant similar facilities for house purchase and, as an alternative, offer endowment loans. Borrowers on this basis can pay up insurance policies over the years and use the maturity proceeds to repay the debts.

House-builders are among the main borrowers from the banks and cheques in settlement of the purchase prices of new properties are paid into their accounts. Consequently, borrowing from building societies often reduces bank lending. Again, personal borrowing replaces corporate finance.

In regard to (b), it should be noted that nothing is actually paid into the current account or withdrawn from the debtor one at this stage. Again, this form of book-keeping suits the banks, but makes a mockery of the notion that all deposits are 'money'. When they lend, the banks release basic money supply credits, which is why, in the event of a run, they would not be able to repay all their depositors. There is, of course, no good reason why such a run should take place, as the shortage of immediately available funds only arises because depositors are not usually called upon to make advance or stage payments in respect of debts being incurred and the goods they will purchase.

Every business operates on the basis that its daily cash flow, in and out, is small in relation to its assets and liabilities. None could repay its debts at once. In perspective, therefore, the position of the banks is not unusual.

Borrowing by short term fixtures or term loans is also posted to creditor accounts. Thus, while basic money supply credits are released, a vast deception is practised upon themselves by those who believe that bank deposits continue to be 'money'. It cannot be repeated too often; they are bank records.

There is a flow of funds into accounts in respect of payments made by the banks on their own behalf for normal outgoings and other items, such as dividends. To meet bank charges, the main borrowers have to sell goods and services to the depositors and, as they do so, funds flow in their direction. Payment of their charges results in funds coming into the banks' possession on their own account. As the banks' retained profits are invested, the outgoing and incoming flows must on average be about equal.

The overall picture is one of funds being pushed through the system in constantly similar patterns and the reality is very different from the concept of banks creating credit, and hence money, by lending. It is not a harmful situation.

It is part of the work of cashiers to decide how much cash their branches will need to meet their customers' requirements. There is normally a heavy demand for cash for wages towards the end of each week and most of the funds withdrawn for this purpose come back into the hands of the banks via shops at the beginning of the following week. Withdrawals are heavier than normal during the holiday season and at Christmas time. A pattern soon emerges and cashiers are able to estimate the amount of cash they will require in any given week.

Those branches with too much cash remit the surplus to their Head Offices, or branches and departments set up to handle cash remittances, and those in need of cash obtain their requirements from these sources. Net surplus notes are paid into the Bank of England and net surplus coin is returned to the Royal Mint, with the appropriate sums in both cases being credited to the accounts maintained by the banks with the Bank of England. Equally, when more notes and coin are needed, they are drawn from those institutions at the debit of the accounts.

It should be noted that the cashiers are not concerned with the ratios which the cash bears to the deposits at their branches and simply have to ensure that they hold enough cash on hand at all times to cover outgoings. If the cash to deposits ratios were calculated, they would vary widely from branch to branch and from day to day, though the average for the banks as a whole usually works out at around eight per cent, when calculated at the close of business on the third Wednesday of each month, which is the date of the banks' monthly balance.

Lending at branch level usually falls into the province of bank managers. It is normal for them to be given limits which vary with the individual and the size of the branch, up to which they can authorise loans and beyond which they have to obtain sanction from their Head Offices. In addition, they receive instructions from time to time to ensure that they comply with any official regulations which may be in force. They are not, however, concerned with 'the pyramid of credit'. Thus, they do not have to calculate liquidity ratios to ensure that any proposed borrowing fits into such a pyramid nor have to worry in case the withdrawal of cash will bring one crashing down.

Bankers have learned from experience how to conduct their businesses to the best advantage. In carrying out their well-tried practices, they ensure that an adequate supply of media of exchange is available at all times and that the flows of funds can proceed without hindrance.

As we have seen, funds placed with a bank, which depositors have no intention of spending, are in a dormant state and out of use. They have been received as service credits, but, in respect of them, reciprocal services cannot be performed by service debtors. The need is not to create more 'money', but to get the use of the dormant funds. Bank lending meets that need, either by financing the production of goods and the provision of services, or by making the funds available to parties who wish to live beyond their immediate means. It bridges the gap and matches underspending with over-spending.

Another point to note is that the more funds banks lend, the easier they make it for their existing borrowers to repay their loans.

The growth in trading activity and settlement procedures

When basic money is created, it is essential that it should remain in existence until the service debtors are ready to redeem their debts. We need, therefore, to look at the ways in which this can be done.

Basic money, as we have observed, came into being when man first agreed to perform a service on condition that a reciprocal one would be carried out in return. Thus, the earliest basic money was made up entirely of verbal promises.

A society basing its trade solely on barter has never been a realistic concept, for man's needs do not match up completely with those of his fellows, either in quantity or on time scale. Consequently, basic money has always been required to bridge the gaps. If our farmer had lived in a society where only barter took place, he would not have been able to acquire a horse and his crop would not have been reaped in full. Yet unless the wheat was harvested, the community could have starved. Do we really believe that the horse would not have been sold against a promise to deliver a quantity of wheat? No? Then basic money would have been created in the barter society.

Initially, trade was conducted on a local basis between people who knew one another. Gradually it expanded to take in neighbouring tribes and eventually became the worldwide business we know today. Barter transactions and basic money creation by promises still take place in the modern world, but they were not enough to cope with the growing trade. These promises are, however, the rudiments of the monetary system, which has become more sophisticated with every step along the way in order to facilitate trade, meet convenience and improve efficiency. Nevertheless, the principles of basic money creation and destruction remain the same throughout all time.

Thus, the process is entirely separate from the methods of transferring the ownership or possession of the basic money supply credits. Media of exchange, book-keeping and bank lending are not features of the process of the creation and destruction of basic money. They are developments which have taken place in the settlement and banking systems.

In the course of history, persons of standing, such as merchants, landowners, goldsmiths, bankers, princes and kings, were able to issue their own markers for making purchases or granting loans. Other people used these markers as trading counters with the result that, at any given time, many had not been presented for redemption. An outstanding amount of basic money, ever-changing in its constituents, was thus kept in existence.

The introduction of cheques increased the number of parties able to issue their own markers. Moreover, bank cheque cards in support made these markers more acceptable. Cheques issued by a service creditor are paid on presentation to the drawee bank. Payment has been made in services and the relevant account now reflects this state of affairs.

A bank buys the cheques of its borrowing customers on presentation, just as someone in the past might have purchased an IOU, and uses depositors' funds for the purpose. Instead of holding onto the cheques until they are redeemed, it debits them to an overdrawn account and offsets the balance with any incoming funds. Thus, a bank could have done the same for our impecunious farmer if his cheque had been accepted in payment for the horse, and he could have cleared his borrowing from the proceeds of the sale of wheat.

We can use the farmer's purchase of the horse in further illustration of the fact that the process of basic money creation and destruction is entirely separate from the methods of settlement by assuming that the transaction takes place in differing sets of circumstances. Already we have seen what would happen in a barter society in a situation where a simple promise was acceptable, and in one where a personal marker was issued.

Now we can consider third party markers. Assume that when the farmer contacts the horse-seller, the latter refuses to take a personal marker. The farmer has no present means of making payment, so he calls on the local baron and seeks his assistance.

On the basis that the sack of wheat is worth two units of their currency, the baron gives the farmer his note for 200 units. We shall ignore any interest element, as it is not essential to the argument. As always, the lending has no effect on the basic money supply.

The farmer hands the note to the horse-seller, who is a service creditor. Basic money has been created by the farmer's debtor spending on the horse-seller's creditor services.

The latter uses the note to make purchases from the baron, who is also a service creditor. Basic money is unchanged in amount, but the constituent parts of the basic money supply credits have been altered.

The credit element has been negotiated, but while the debt appears to be that of the baron, it is actually the farmer's. He used the baron's note as his personal marker. The position would have been the same had the baron written a guarantee on a marker issued by the farmer. In relation to the creation of basic money, it is the farmer's marker and not the baron's.

In redeeming his own note, the baron bought the farmer's marker. He now stands in the place of the horse-seller and keeps the basic money in existence by allowing the farmer the agreed time at the end of which to effect settlement. In due course, the farmer delivers the wheat to the baron and asks for a receipt. The baron hands him the note and invites him to destroy it.

Nowadays, service creditors and service debtors use banknotes and coin as their personal markers respectively to reduce their credits and to increase their debts. Thus, we confirm that all 'modern money' is *not* the liability of financial organisations.

The horse-seller could have insisted on payment in cash issued by the state. Our impecunious farmer would have had to borrow a sum equal to the purchase price. He would then use state media of exchange as his own markers. It would be just as if his markers were guaranteed by the state. Basic money would still have been created by the farmer's debtor spending on creditor services and not by the state.

In theory at least, the farmer could have acquired the horse and used a credit card for settlement purposes. The seller would obtain payment from the credit card company. That organisation would keep the debt, and hence basic money, in existence by posting the price to a debtor account. Thus, it would have bought the farmer's marker in the same way as a bank would, had he issued a cheque.

The obsession with 'the creation of credit' has led us to believe that increases in bank lending and credit card transactions are harmful. This is not the case. Anything which facilitates trade is to our advantage, provided always that parties do not overcommit themselves.

We have, of course, always classed cash as 'money' and no doubt will continue so doing. Nevertheless, this is an inadequate description. Notes and coin in use are titles to basic money supply credits and are better described as 'nominal money'. They stand in relation to such credits as title-deeds do to houses. Thus, they are instruments for evidencing the creation, destruction, transfer or lending of the credits.

A marker has to be acceptable to the party to whom it is offered, to a further party if it is to be negotiated and to parties in general if it is to go into regular use. In Britain, notes and coin issued respectively by the Bank of England and the Royal Mint are media of exchange of the state, as these two organisations are its agents. Notes and coin are acceptable to parties in general and go into use to the extent that the public wishes to have them. Cash in use represents an interest-free loan to the state. In practice, however, this is not a separate spendable sum; it simply reduces the total borrowing needed to finance the state's transactions.

Cheques issued by government departments are usually drawn on Bank of England accounts. Those drawn on creditor accounts are paid on presentation to the central bank, but those drawn on debtor accounts are kept in existence by being posted in the computerised ledger. Thus, like any other bank, the Bank of England prevents the markers of its debtor customers from being presented for immediate redemption.

Many people borrow funds from building societies for house purchase. Their debts are kept in existence by the societies and are reduced gradually by the payment of regular instalments. Thus, the principles are the same regardless of the nature of the lending organisation.

Banks lend state markers when cash is borrowed from them, and buy their debtor customers' cheques. The first action lends basic money supply credits, while the second keeps basic money supply debts in existence.

The state of development in a society is determined by the ability of its members to trade. This inevitably means that some parties will perform services for others on the understanding that reciprocal ones will be obtainable. In the early stages the service debtor wipes out his obligation by carrying out his part of the bargain, but in the later ones the reciprocal service may be performed for any service creditor or another service debtor.

Basic money creation and destruction occur outside the banking system. The records of the banks and other deposit-takers duly reflect the changing involvement of their customers in the trading transactions.

As already stated, the bilateral definition of basic money supply is the total value of the service credits not yet spent, measured in a unit of account, or the total amount of the service debts not yet redeemed, also so measured.

Differing values can be given to the unit of account, but the services have been performed and are unalterable. Variations in such values take place outside the banking system and cause distortions in the economy, such as inflation and deflation. Basic money would otherwise be a very precise means of settlement. It has been contended that there is a monetary phenomenon, but that is simply not the case. Basic money has been blamed wrongly for the faults and weaknesses of people.

Fortunately, no unilateral creation of basic money takes place in, or is generated by, the banking system; indeed, nothing happening within that system can affect the value of money, basic or nominal. There are, therefore, only two ways in which basic money can be increased: (1) by inflation and (2) by more trading activity. The former is damaging and requires to be dealt with by governmental action, but the latter is healthy and should be encouraged. Recovery and growth cannot take place without an increase in real terms in the basic money supply.

A great amount of time and effort have been wasted on attempts to measure the 'money supply' and considerable damage has been inflicted on the economy by policies based upon the results. The basic money supply is self-regulating, is not a catalyst in any way and, in the absence of inflation and deflation, would simply reflect the level of trading activity in the community. It cannot be used successfully as an economic indicator nor can it function as a lever.

Maximum economic progress is made by a country when all its inhabitants are able to trade or, in other words, there is full employment. The true measures of a nation's health are, therefore, the level of trading activity, the maintenance of full employment and the absence of inflation and deflation, except in the processes of correction.

Whether we like it or not, pay and price levels are the keys to the economy because they are the factors which affect the values and burdens of basic money. The values are determined by the purchasing power, on average, of the new basic money supply credits being created; indeed, the values of the outstanding basic money supply credits automatically come into line with those of the new ones. The basic money supply debts are affected in step, the basis being: less value, less burden – more value, more burden. The way to control a currency's value is, therefore, to adjust the pay and price structure in whatever direction is needed to achieve that end.

Custodians and lenders

On page 48, it was shown that funds flow into the hands of deposit-takers as deposits and repayments and out as withdrawals and loans. The funds, rising and falling in amount, are going round in a circle and an illustration of the process appears on page 49.

Such deposit-takers, in the course of these operations, are conducting two separate businesses, the resulting figures for which are amalgamated. The first is as custodians for the deposits of their creditor customers and the second as lenders meeting the needs of their borrowers.

A bank acting as custodian provides for withdrawals by way of cash or by payment of cheques. The transactions are for the purpose of creditor spending. If the spending is on creditor services, old basic money supply credits are destroyed and new ones are created; their values are paid into the banking system as new deposits. If the spending is on debtor services, basic money supply is destroyed; the sums involved are paid into the banking system as repayment of debt.

Because all the depositors do not wish to withdraw their funds at the same time and use less than eight per cent of them, on average, in any one day, the deposit-takers are able to lend the rest for the purpose of debtor spending.

It is easy to see that in the case of creditor spending, either on creditor or debtor services, the basic money supply credits involved are destroyed. The picture in relation to those borrowed for debtor spending, however, is not so clear.

All payments have to be made with basic money supply credits. If the spending is on debtor services, old basic money supply debts are destroyed and new ones are created: the sums involved are paid into the banking system as repayment of debt; the basic money supply credits borrowed are returned to the banking system and can be lent again. If the debtor spending is on creditor services, basic money supply is created; the values of the new basic money supply credits are paid into the banking system as deposits; the old basic money supply credits have been destroyed by the spending and their values are owed to the lenders. Put another way, the media of exchange involved in the transactions change on delivery from representing old basic money supply credits to representing new ones. The old credits can be said to be out on rent and all advances are covered in that way.

All transactions settled within the banking system have, therefore, been accounted for and there is clearly no way in which banks can 'create credit, and hence money, by lending'.

The Basic Money Rental Company!

As we now know, basic money is subject to continuous creation and destruction in accordance with the status rules; in terms of those parameters, therefore, it does not circulate. When, however, something has been created, it can be lent – and basic money supply credits are no exception. Accordingly, to the extent of their lending, banks can be said to circulate or recirculate basic money supply credits.

The precise situation in regard to bank lending can be made clear by way of analogy. Cars are manufactured and scrapped; the comparable processes are the creation and destruction of basic money. Some cars are acquired by garages and rented out; the banks collect basic money supply credits and lend most of them. The rented cars are continually returned to the garages; basic money supply credits lent for debtor spending on debtor services return to the banks as repayment of debt. Some new cars are acquired, but the ones on loan are still out; basic money supply credits lent for debtor spending on creditor services return to the banks as deposits, but their values are still owing. No creation of cars or basic money is due to the renting or the lending practices. Remember, too, that the process by which basic money is destroyed – creditor spending on debtor services – is going on at the same time and is equivalent to the scrapping of cars. Rent and interest are the respective charges of the two businesses.

Now, dear reader, whenever you visit your bank or building society, a little smile may cross your lips as you realise that you are in the premises of a basic money rental company!

The Bank of England is no exception!

Parameters

The basic money supply is the result of our actions in trading our services and reflects precisely what we have done in this regard in terms of the unit of account. The process is very efficient. In particular, it allows production to be financed without advance or stage payments having to be made by the ultimate consumers and permits many parties to live beyond their means. Nevertheless, some parameters imposed by the nature of basic money fall to be considered.

Demand for borrowing is usually strong, so the funds available for lending tend to be fully utilised and are always limited in amount. The proliferation of deposits hides the fact that there is a hard core. These are the basic deposits and are comprised solely of the basic money supply credits held by the banking system. The rest, remember, are made up of entries of no value other than for record and accounting purposes, ie, the froth.

Although the basic money supply is intangible, the credits can, as we have seen, be lent and borrowed in the same way as any article or commodity. Moreover, the effect is identical. There is no increase in quantity from such actions and the depositor and the borrower cannot both simultaneously use the same basic money supply credits; equally, if a car is rented, the owner and the hirer cannot use the vehicle for different purposes at the same time. There is only one distinction: the hirer has to return the vehicle in question, but a borrower can repay with any funds he can acquire.

More investment involves additional borrowing, either from the banks or from the public. There are no extra basic money supply credits to finance such projects, so they can only be accommodated at the expense of existing borrowing. In the same way, the introduction of new products can only be made by replacing old ones. Purchasing power is insufficient to buy both. New companies tend to destroy old ones or fail themselves.

The essential features of basic money

Most of the essential features of money – basic and nominal – have now been discussed. They are not going to change for, by the nature of things, they cannot. No doubt there will be further developments in the monetary and banking systems, but, nevertheless, the basic principles will remain unaltered.

No party can throw a stone into the pond of the banking system without creating a ripple of repercussions. Unilateral action is simply not possible and any arguments based upon it, such as that banks can create money by lending, must inevitably be unsound. This is both an economic law and a double-entry accounting one!

3

The Basic Money Supply

Evidence of holdings of basic money

The basic money supply is defined on page 6 as the total value of
the service credits not yet spent, measured in the unit of account; or
the total amount of the service debts, not yet redeemed, also so
measured. Total service credits always equal total service debts; in
other words, savings always equal borrowings.

Owing to the intangible nature of basic money, service creditors
need evidence of their holdings of basic money supply credits. This
they obtain by holding part in media of exchange, such as cash,
cheques, luncheon vouchers, gift tokens and money orders, by
placing part with banks, building societies and other licensed
deposit-takers and by making financial investments. In contrast, any
such items held by service debtors are evidence of offset against
indebtedness.

Can the basic money supply be measured?

Monetarists believe that the quantity of 'money' affects the behaviour of the economy and attempt to measure it with monetary
aggregates, such as cash in circulation and total deposits. They are

trying to discover how much purchasing power there is in the economy, but the methods they are using are unsound and based on misconceptions. They give grossly exaggerated amounts in respect of the purchasing power of cash and deposits. The answers are best described as 'false money supply'.

In considering the question of measurement we, too, can look initially at cash and deposits, but only to the extent that they represent basic money supply credits.

Ian is a service creditor. He holds £56.25 in cash and has £500 in his bank account. When he draws cash he is *purchasing* state media of exchange. His service credits can be measured by adding his holding of cash and his bank balance, ie, £556.25.

John is a service debtor. He holds £39.75 in cash and has an overdraft of £500. When he draws cash, he is *borrowing* state media of exchange. His obligation in service debts can be measured by deducting his holding of cash from his bank balance, ie, debtor £460.25.

Parties can, as appropriate, measure their service credits or service debts. Cash, however, changes sides according to the status of the holder. It is nominal, and not basic, money. Consequently, cash in circulation cannot soundly be used as a collective measure of basic money supply or purchasing power.

By debiting John's account for the cash withdrawn, the bank has anticipated his spending. He could crystallise his position by paying the cash back in.

Deposits, too, are unsuitable as collective measures. Many of the reasons were discussed in Chapter Two in the section headed 'Differences between deposits and basic money'.

One cannot store something which is intangible, so titles to it and records of its movements have to be kept. Under present conditions, however, these records can never be up to date as the alterations take place at the point of delivery. Remember, also, that the banks deal only in *titles* to basic money supply credits.

There are a few examples of instant amendment to the records, such as when a bank credits or debits interest to an account. The point of delivery and the posting of the entry have coincided.

As already noted, the same deposit can appear in more than one set of books and can be counted more than once. In the United States of America, Peter borrows $500 from Robert in the form of five $100 bills. Before he can spend them, Robert asks for repayment. Peter repays Robert and borrows a similar sum from Samuel. None of the official measures have been altered, so not even an economist would maintain that money had been created by the lending. The relevant part of the 'money supply' is $500.

Alter the example. Robert pays the original bills into his deposit account and Peter obtains a loan from the bank involved. By chance, he is given the same bills.

In both cases, nothing material to the economy has changed, but deposits plus cash are now $1,000. On these flimsy grounds, the economic profession would have us believe (a) that the bank, by granting credit, created 'money'; (b) that the 'additional' funds are competing with the original ones; (c) that the process causes inflation and (d) that the increase in 'money supply' is the proof!

In truth, all deposits and loans are subject to the same principles as Robert's $500. They are redispositions. Thus, neither the movement of funds to the banking system, nor the subsequent lending, has any effect on the basic money supply. When a bank is interposed, service credits are double-counted.

If Robert spends his $500, Peter's loan is covered by the deposits of someone else, in other words another Samuel.

Suppose that Robert deposits his $500 with a small bank which, in turn, pays this cash into a larger bank – the American system – and that Peter obtains the same bills from the latter. The nightmare worsens! Cash plus two deposits now total $1,500! 'Money supply' is now triple-counted!

Robert's deposit is surplus to local needs and is transferred across the country from bank to bank until it reaches the main financial centre, New York. There it is lent as part of the facilities granted to a major borrower. It can never be more than $500.

In Britain, the banking system transfers the surplus deposits directly to London, so double-counting is probably the worst situation here.

We can now consider other financial holdings for inclusion in, or exclusion from, calculations.

It is correct to include liquid assets, such as government securities at cost. These assets represent the borrowing of the state of basic money supply credits from the public.

At present, stocks and shares are not included in 'money supply' calculations. A question arises. Is a company in issuing stocks and shares borrowing? Legally, the shareholders become the owners of the company, but in practice the company uses the shareholders' funds to purchase assets on its own account. It is, therefore, borrowing. The basis is virtually permanent. Stocks and shares are borrowing instruments of companies in the same way as gilt-edged securities are of the state. They should be included at cost in 'money supply' calculations. There is no difference in principle.

Endowment policies are another form of borrowing and investment. The issuers borrow the instalments for their own purposes and repay the accrued sums plus bonuses on the due dates. Any financial asset which represents borrowing should be included. The transactions are all redispositions and do not affect the statuses of the participants.

Foreign currencies represent parts of the basic money supplies of other nations and are held as deposits in banks *abroad*. It is wrong to add in their sterling equivalents, as home balances owned by foreigners are already included. Consider a simplified example involving two depositors, one on each side of the Atlantic. Hank, a New Yorker, exchanges US$15,000 for £10,000 owned by Arnold, a Londoner. If foreign currency deposits are included in 'money supply' calculations, double-counting takes place; in the United States Arnold's US$15,000 plus the dollar equivalent of £10,000, in Britain Hank's £10,000 plus the sterling equivalent of US$15,000. Hank's £10,000 should, therefore, be included in our 'money supply' calculations and Arnold's US$15,000 in those of the United States.

The basic money supply is that part of a nation's wealth which is held in financial form. Measuring it on a total basis is presently impossible, but it can be calculated for any party on a single basis.

Service creditors can calculate their shares of the basic money supply by adding together cash in hand, deposits and financial investments at cost. The total of these positions is the correct answer for the basic money supply.

Service debtors can calculate the extent of their service debts by deducting their holdings of the following items from their gross indebtedness: cash in hand, deposits and financial investments at cost. The total of these positions then also gives the correct answer for the basic money supply. Total service credits always equal total service debts. It is impossible to devise a transaction which defeats this equation. Moreover, this has been the situation since primitive man first advanced beyond barter.

Fortunately, there is no need to measure the basic money supply as it is self-regulating. Every transaction obeys the status rules. Further, the basic money supply is the *result* of the trading activity in the community and not a catalyst which can affect the economy.

The Mystery of the Vanishing Money Supply

This is the mystery mentioned in the Introduction to this book. It is time to consider it in full and to present the solution.

On 28 April 1993, I submitted the following hypothesis to the Bank of England and asked for confirmation that my contentions were correct:

> Suppose that Britain became a cashless society and that the notes and coin in circulation were paid into accounts with banks and building societies. Savers would increase their deposits; borrowers would reduce their indebtedness to lenders.
>
> The cash would be returned to the Bank of England and in redemption exchanged for the government securities presently held in cover of the note and coin issues. Bankers' Deposits at the Bank would not, therefore, increase.
>
> The money supply (taken here as cash plus deposits) would fall! Moreover, since the main suppliers of goods and services, such as industry and shops, are bank borrowers, the fall would be substantial.
>
> Where would the difference in purchasing power have gone?

Nowhere. No party would lose purchasing power, so the difference does not exist. The correct count for MO is cash in circulation less cash in the hands of borrowers.

The Bank did not dispute the envisaged sequence of events, but thought that, '...the suggestion that MO should be measured net of cash holdings of borrowers is not obviously theoretically appropriate or practically applicable'.

True, cash in the hands of borrowers cannot be measured, but that does not invalidate the arguments. The discrepancy in MO is much too important to be ignored and the principle also applies to the rest of the monetary aggregates. Financial assets in the hands of borrowers fall to be deducted from gross totals of indebtedness.

It remained for me to submit the proof of my contentions to the Bank. In this connection, I would mention that I had not yet decided to classify money as basic and nominal and usually used the term 'real money' to describe the former. Here is a brief version of the proof submitted.

In a primitive society, A performs a service for B on the understanding that the latter will perform a reciprocal one at a later date. Money has been *created*; it is a credit *in services* of one party and a debt *in services* of another. B duly performs the reciprocal service; money has been *destroyed*. Thus, money is subject to a process of continuous creation and destruction.

As trade developed, many parties (individuals and groups) moved into credit in terms of services (service creditors) and the rest (service debtors) got into debt to the same extent. The transactions then became so intertwined that the credits and debts became respectively due from and to the community in general, rather than from and to specific parties. Nevertheless, total service credits always equal total service debts and the real money supply is either total.

It became desirable to have evidence that the credits and debts existed, to value them in common denominators and to have an intervening device which would allow the services to be exchanged at the times and in the proportions wanted. Money was then defined as anything which acts as a medium of exchange, a unit of account or a store of value.

Thus, this definition completely ignored the true nature of money and, in particular, the fact that it is two-sided, a credit and a debt. Moreover, it made the rational discussion of 'money' extremely difficult. To remedy this, I informed the Bank that I would use 'money' in its accepted sense and 'basic or real money' to refer to the credits and debts in services. Money then becomes a title to basic money in the same way as a title-deed does to a house. Basic money is the real money, just as the house is the real property.

Distinction has to be made between the trading activity (the process by which real money is created and destroyed) and the settlement procedures (the use of media of exchange, accounts, etc). Thus, real money relates to the former, while money (the titles) is part of the latter.

A further distinction has to be made between transactions which involve the performance of work and those which are purely financial. The former affect the economy, while the latter do not. Thus, depositing, borrowing, currency exchange and other movements of titles to real money would be irrelevant, but for the fact that they facilitate trade. Financial markets deal in titles to real money; they do not create it. Banks, too, only create money by spending themselves into debt in terms of services, and not by lending. The raising of capital from the public is a purely financial transaction and the subsequent spending of it makes most organisations service debtors.

The basic situation demonstrated in the example of A and B is unalterable and must always apply in trading activities. Everything else post-barter, from cowrie shells via tobacco, gold and banknotes to modern technology, is simply a development which has made the dealings of the As and Bs of this world, whether individuals or groups, more convenient and more efficient. Thus, they are still the ones who create and destroy real money.

The reason as to why the correct count for MO is cash in circulation less cash in the hands of borrowers can now be given. Because of the two-sided nature of real money, both the credits and the debts have to be represented by titles which prove how the transactions stand. For example, in the case of A and B, the latter could have given the former an IOU and got it back on completion of the reciprocal service. In A's hands the title would show that the debt was due and real money created, whereas back in B's possession it would prove that the debt had been redeemed and real money destroyed. When a third-party IOU, such as a banknote, is used, the effect is the same.

Cash in circulation and the other monetary aggregates are not, therefore, suitable criteria for measuring purchasing power.

A realistic formula, in accounting terms, for measuring the real money supply would be as follows:

Service Credits – £billions		*Service Debts – £billions*		
(held by service creditors only)		Gross Indebtedness		£2,220
Cash	£ 60	*less* Cash	40	
Deposits	920	Deposits	80	
Investments	1,020	Investments	100	220
	£2,000			£2,000

The figures are for demonstration purposes only. All other assets of a purely financial nature are included in Investments except foreign currencies, which are titles to the real money of other nations.

It is impossible to devise a transaction which unbalances this equation. Indeed, this has been the situation since primitive man first advanced beyond barter.

A banknote is a purchasing voucher bought from the Bank for general purchases, in the same way as a luncheon voucher, bought from the issuer, is for a specific one. In calculating the number of meals which can be purchased, vouchers already honoured by restaurants have to be deducted from those in circulation. The same principle applies to banknotes. If luncheon vouchers were reusable, the comparison would match completely.

Assume that when Britain became a cashless society the country was on the Gold Standard and that the currency consisted entirely of gold coins. Deposits would rise, advances would fall and the Bank would exchange government securities for the gold. The position would be the same as with a paper currency.

It is quite wrong, therefore, to believe that if the country were on the Gold Standard purchasing power would equal the total of the coins in circulation. The correct count would be coins in circulation less those in the hands of borrowers (service debtors). Even a gold coin can never be more than a title to real money.

Banknotes can have a velocity of circulation, but real money can only be used once. That is the experience of us all and the economy is the sum total of those experiences. Each movement of a banknote relates to a different transaction.

A borrower incurs two debts, one to the lender in terms of cash and the other, on spending, to the community in terms of services. The latter has to be redeemed by the performance of reciprocal services in order to obtain the funds to repay the former. Thus, it is the second debt which affects the economy, whereas the first is simply a private arrangement. Real money is not created by bank lending, but by parties spending themselves into debt in terms of services.

Raw materials and produce are provided free by nature. Consequently, it is only the services involved in production and supply that are paid for and are recouped by the sale of goods. The material element is always passed on without charge. Thus, it is not goods and services which are being exchanged, but services only. The concurrent creation of material wealth is a by-product of the trading system in services.

My correspondence with the Bank covered a period of six months and included the submission of the accounting formula. Payments from service debtors to service creditors increase the real money supply and both sides of the equation, while those in the reverse direction have the opposite effects.

The Bank wrote, '...we are not interested in the money supply *per se* but in what it can tell us about the demand for liquidity in the economy'.

Real money supply and liquidity are, however, two different things. Deposits turn over continuously at varying rates, but the great majority of them represent funds the owners have no immediate intention of spending, which is why they can be borrowed. Advances, too, are turning over, but the major part is needed to cover existing borrowing and is not available for spending. True liquidity in the economy is, therefore, the part of deposits the owners intend to spend plus the part still available to borrowing spenders. The M measures do not measure real money supply or liquidity and can be of no practical use. In any event, the real money supply is self-regulating and it is pointless to try to measure it.

Nevertheless, in closing the correspondence, the Bank averred, '...we do believe that these aggregates contain useful information and we are therefore keen to use them as indicators of both current and future economic conditions'.

Originally, I sought the Bank's confirmation of the contentions in my hypothesis, but, although I proved my points, this was not forthcoming.

In reinforcement of the comments on the behaviour of cash, (the IOU in the case of A and B), it can be noted that a banknote in the hands of a service creditor is a title to purchasing power; if spent on creditor services, it continues to be such a title; but if spent on debtor services, it changes to evidence that reciprocal services have been performed and basic money has been destroyed. A banknote in the hands of a service debtor for expenditure is a title to borrowed purchasing power; if spent on creditor services, it becomes a title to purchasing power and shows that basic money has been created: but if spent on debtor services, it changes to evidence that reciprocal services have been performed, though basic money in total is unchanged. In the last event, the new debt of the spender has replaced the old debt of the recipient. The banknote, however, is in the latter's hands, so it represents an offset against indebtedness rather than purchasing power. Since most of the shops are bank borrowers, the banknote would now probably be on its way back to the banking system as part of the inward cash flow, which reduces borrowing. Its situation is, therefore, the same as if it had been spent by a service creditor on debtor services. In a correct calculation of M0 to ascertain purchasing power, banknotes in the hands of service debtors fall to be deducted from the total in circulation, as the hypothesis contends.

In short, cash circulates, but, as seen from the experiences of A and B, its passing has different results. 'Thus, it keeps changing character, back and forth, sometimes representing purchasing power and, for the rest, being evidence of offset against indebtedness, according to whether it is in the hands of a service creditor or a service debtor.

The two-sided nature of basic money shows up best in the double-entry book-keeping system used by British banks. Payments from borrowers (on the assets side of balance sheets) to depositors (on the liabilities side) show that the basic money supply has been increased and those in the reverse direction that it has been reduced. The rest, between parties of like status, show that the constituent parts of the basic money supply have been altered, though its totals remain unchanged. Total service credits always equal total service debts. The actions of the service creditors affect the credits and those of the service debtors the debts. These are unilateral actions, but it is the joint effect which determines the quantity of basic money.

In the Introduction, it was noted that, under an American banking system, overdrawn positions are not permitted and loans are credited to accounts. If a society in which this system were in operation became cashless, the notes and coin would be paid entirely into creditor accounts and it would appear that the money supply was unaffected. No part of it would vanish. A further explanation is, therefore, required.

If Luke borrows US$10,000, he is in debt when his balance is below this sum to the extent of the difference. A net outflow from accounts in that position reflects an increase in the basic money supply and a net inflow a reduction. Thus, the principles are the same regardless of the banking system. In the British one, the process is visible, while in the American one, it is not. Nevertheless, it is still there.

Redemption of the American currency would cause an inflow into the creditor accounts of both savers and borrowers. In the case of the savers, the additional deposits would reflect the purchasing power of their cash holdings, whereas in respect of the borrowers they would evidence the offset against indebtedness.

It can be noted that the proliferation of deposits is greater in the USA than in Britain! The calculation of money supply there as cash plus deposits is, therefore, even more unsound.

In regard to 'money', Americans have a saying, 'What goes round comes round'. They believe that basic money simply circulates. We, on the other hand, now know that it is subject to a process of continuous creation and destruction and that it is cash (nominal money), which circulates, or, in more accurate terms, can be reused.

Perhaps the Federal Reserve Bank will welcome this information and the Bank of England will see the need to alter its stance.

The Accounting Formula

Some readers, particularly those who have studied monetary theory, may be having difficulty in accepting my contentions in replacement of traditional teaching. It remains for me, therefore, to hammer home the facts with a practical and irrefutable demonstration.

Let me begin with an extract from the section headed 'Can the basic money supply be measured?', earlier in this chapter.

> The basic money supply is that part of a nation's wealth, which is held in financial form. Measuring it on a total basis is presently impossible, but it can be calculated for any party on a single basis.
>
> Service creditors can calculate their shares of the basic money supply by adding together cash in hand, deposits and financial investments at cost. The total of these positions is the correct answer for the basic money supply.
>
> Service debtors can calculate the extent of their service debts by deducting their holdings of the following items from their gross indebtedness: Cash in hand, deposits and financial investments at cost. The total of these positions then also gives the correct answer for the basic money supply. Total service credits always equal total service debts.

When valued in a unit of account, this means that total savings always equal total borrowings. In passing, we can note, therefore, that there is no special merit in savings. Indeed, the owners have no option but to hold their financial wealth in the forms of cash, deposits and investments.

The realistic formula, now slightly amended, for measuring the basic money supply, if it were possible, would be as follows:

Service Credits – £billions			*Service Debts – £billions*		
(held by service creditors only)			Gross Indebtedness		£2,290
Cash	£	60	*less* Cash	40	
Deposits		990	Deposits	80	
Investments		1,020	Investments	100	220
		£2,070			£2,070
less Debts		70	*less* Credits		70
		£2,000			£2,000

The figures are for demonstration purposes only. Liquid assets (government debt) and stocks and shares (company debt) are included in Investments. Other purely financial assets, such as endowment policies, should be regarded as similarly classified at cost. Foreign currency holdings are excluded as they are parts of the basic money supplies of other nations, but sterling balances owned by foreigners are included in Deposits. Gross Indebtedness includes the National Debt.

All service creditors have some outstanding debts and Deposits could be deemed to include an amount in cover. I have, however, felt it desirable to make the position more explicit. Accordingly, I have amended the original version of the formula by increasing Deposits and providing a compensating deduction for Debts. In a similar way, all service debtors have some funds due to them for services performed for which they have not yet been paid. I have, therefore, increased Gross Indebtedness and provided a compensating deduction for such credits. Readers should bear in mind that the credits and debts are created and destroyed by the performance of services, whereas settlement lags behind.

In its present form, the formula should be used for testing large transactions, but for smaller ones it can be regarded as being in

£millions, £thousands or simply pounds. No transaction or event can cause it to go out of balance.

The value of the formula lies in the facts that (1) the effect of any transaction can be revealed by it and (2) the efficacy of any monetary concept can be judged against it. Here is an example.

Do banks create money by lending? Archie, a service debtor, borrows £30 in cash from his bank – no effect. Gross Indebtedness rises, but so does the Cash Deduction, both on the Service Debts side. Bank lending has not created basic money. Archie pays £30 to his dentist, who has a creditor bank balance. Service Credits and Service Debts increase to the same extent. Basic money is, therefore, created by debtor spending on creditor services and destroyed by creditor spending on debtor services. The process by which basic money is created is wrongly being attributed to bank lending and the one by which it is destroyed is being ignored.

It remains, therefore, to test the contentions by considering the effects of some further examples under three sub-headings: (1) trading transactions, (2) financial dealings and (3) outside events.

Trading transactions
(a) A service debtor company pays wages to its service creditor employees; payment is made from the company's overdraft and the funds are credited to the employees' accounts. The rise in Deposits on the Credits side is matched by the increase in Gross Indebtedness. Both totals go up to the same extent. Basic money has been created.

(b) A service creditor buys goods or services from a service debtor and pays in cash. The fall in Cash Credits is matched by the increase in the Cash Deduction from Gross Indebtedness. Both totals go down to an equal extent. Basic money has been destroyed.

(c) A service creditor buys goods or services from another service creditor and pays by cheque. The first party's Deposits fall, while the second's rise equally. The buyer spends some credits; the seller creates new ones to the same extent. Thus, although total basic money is unaffected, every transaction alters its constituent parts.

(d) A service debtor buys goods or services from another service debtor and pays with borrowed cash. Total basic money supply is unaffected. The increase in Gross Indebtedness is matched by the rise in the Cash Deduction. A vast amount of transactions take place between service debtors. It should be noted, therefore, that the widely accepted contention that every loan creates a deposit is not only false, but very wide of the mark.

(e) A service debtor buys foreign currency, say US dollars, from a service creditor. The first party pays the sterling equivalent to the second, thereby creating basic money and causing both sides of the formula to increase equally. The buyer now has a dollar balance in New York made up of funds transferred from the seller's account in that city. Thus, contrary to popular belief, basic money cannot cross borders or change nationality. The effects on the basic money supply of the USA depend on the statuses of the parties in that country. A transaction in the reverse direction – a service creditor buying foreign currency from a service debtor – would destroy basic money here and cause both sides of the formula to fall.

(f) Debts which become irredeemable result in an equal amount of Credits and Debts being wiped out. The loss of purchasing power and lending capability causes the economy to contract. It is not a case of one party's loss being another party's gain.

Financial dealings
(g) A bank gives a borrower a loan of £100 in cash. Basic money supply in total is unaffected. Gross Indebtedness increases, but so does the Cash Deduction. Basic money is not created by bank lending, but by debtor spending on creditor services. This, of course, is the situation noted in Archie's case.

(h) A bank grants a borrower a loan of £500 by cross entry. Thus, it credits this sum to his account and debits it to a new account in his name. If the borrower is a service creditor, Deposits and Debts, both on the Credits side of the formula, increase, leaving total basic money supply unchanged. If the borrower is a service debtor, Gross Indebtedness increases, but so does the Deposits Deduction, leaving total basic money supply unchanged. Again, it is confirmed that bank lending does not increase the basic money supply.

(i) It is necessary to distinguish between direct investments and subsequent dealings. The former are created by (a) buying gilt-edged securities from the government's agents, (b) acquiring new issue or rights offer stocks and shares and (c) engaging in other lending transactions.

Buying and selling stocks and shares are dealings in government and company debt. The sums paid for direct investments are fixed, whereas the subsequent dealings can be for greater or smaller amounts. They are barter transactions, in which one of the assets exchanged is cash. The status rules apply, *but only to the extent that the new prices exceed or fall short of the original ones.*

A service creditor makes a direct investment and pays by cheque. On the Credits side, the increase in Investments is matched by the fall in Deposits while, on the Debts side, the increase in Gross Indebtedness is offset, say, by a rise in the Deposits Deduction. Basic money is unchanged in amount.

A service creditor sells a direct investment of £200 to a service debtor for £500. On the Credits side, Deposits rise by £500, but Investments fall by £200. On the Debts side, Gross Indebtedness increases by £500 and the Investments Deduction by £200. Basic money is up by £300.

The service debtor sells the investment to a service creditor for £800. On the Credits side, Deposits fall by that sum, but Investments rise by £200, while on the Debts side, Gross Indebtedness falls by £800 and the Investments Deduction by £200. Basic money is down by £600.

Suppose instead that the service debtor sells the investment to a service creditor for £150. On the Credits side, Deposits fall by £150 and Investments rise by £200, while on the Debts side, Gross Indebtedness is down by £150 and the Investment Deduction by £200. Basic money is up by £50.

Remember that the debts of the government and the companies are still owing. The difference between selling material assets and existing securities is that, in the first instance, the status rules apply to the whole transaction, but, in the second, not to the direct investment element.

Outside events

(j) Britain becomes cashless. Total basic money supply is unaffected. On the Credits side, the fall in Cash is matched by the increase in Deposits while, on the Debts side, the fall in Gross Indebtedness is offset by the decrease in the Cash Deduction.

(k) Inflation causes the Service Credits to lose purchasing power and makes the Service Debts less burdensome to the same extent. Deflation has the opposite effects.

It has not been possible to measure the basic money supply in total. Benefits, however, arise from knowing how the monetary system works and in being able to test the efficacy of concepts against the formula. Here are three examples.

(1) Interest Rate Adjustments. If interest rates are cut, the reduction in the cost of borrowing is offset by the loss of income of the savers. There is no net benefit to the internal economy. The cost of exports would fall and more would be sold; the benefits, however, would be offset by strengthening exchange rates; imports would be cheaper, but there would be less purchasing power to buy them. Raising interest rates causes the reverse effects. Unilateral monetary policies can never be effective, as there are always repercussions. The function of the interest rates is to hold the ring between the limited supply of funds available for lending and the demand for borrowing. Thus, interest rates should be raised when such demand increases and be reduced in the opposite circumstances. It is a mistake to try to use them for any other purpose.

(2) Capital Gains Tax. In view of the bilateral nature of money, this tax should be reconsidered. Realising profits is a sensible investment decision and should not be penalised by the loss of part of one's capital. Most gains arise from one service creditor selling securities to another, an action which has no effect on the quantity of basic money.

(3) Tessa and Peps. One party's savings is another party's borrowing. Thus, savings have no special merit. There is, therefore, no logic to, or justification for, the tax relief granted under these schemes. In addition, it is wrong for the government to encourage tax avoidance. Another point is that our impecunious Treasury is the service debtor to the tax relief and has to borrow at interest to cover the concessions! In any event, this tax relief is being granted at the expense of more needy citizens and should be cancelled on those grounds alone.

On more general aspects, our understanding of how the monetary system works allows us to assess past events and to note what should have been done.

Bankruptcies, liquidations, major financial losses and increased unemployment, resulting from unsound management decisions, destroyed a large part of our basic money supply, our ability to trade, our lending capacity and our power to generate new funds. These are the factors which caused the recent recession and the reduction in the rate of inflation. The effects can be appreciated by noting in the basic money supply accounting formula that they eliminated a large and equal amount of service credits and service debts. Thus, the economy contracted and was left with insufficient purchasing power to maintain the previous standard of living. A further contributory factor was the loss incurred by the Treasury in its ill-fated attempt to prevent the pound from falling through its lower limit in the Exchange Rate Mechanism.

Although the basic money supply is subject to a process of continuous creation and destruction, there is always an amount outstanding at any given time. One result is that there is a limit on the funds available for lending and it is important that they should be used to the best advantage in the national interest.

Every country needs its own basic money supply to maintain and advance its standard of living. Knowing this, sovereign lending can be seen to be an obvious mistake and, in the event, the damaging losses incurred and the non-performing loans inhibited our own economy.

The housing boom should have been regulated by governmental action and the lending rationed. Thus, for example, if the salary multiple had been restricted to $2\frac{1}{2}$ times, more houses could have been purchased and sold, while prices would have remained stable. A house, after all, is a wasting asset and should only retain its value if fully maintained. As it was, some persons receiving salary increases moved to larger houses irrespective of need. Valuable lending facilities were then used to finance empty rooms. Throwing funds at any market creates a bonanza for sellers at the expense of buyers. The banks and building societies have to compete for deposits and lending, so none was in a position to resist the market forces. Competition does not always favour the buyer.

At the same time, more and more office accommodation was built with little regard to where the people to occupy it were to come from. An excessive amount of funds were provided to the builders of such property. Since the funds available for lending are limited, less were available for other business and personal purposes.

In these circumstances, interest rates were forced up and an unsustainable boom was created.

Savers should be content to preserve their capital and earn interest from it, but instead a truly vast industry has grown up both at home and abroad in financial dealings. A small part is needed to finance trade, but the rest is comprised of gambling transactions. I find it incredible that the G7 finance ministers and central bankers have not seen the need to ban lending for such purposes.

Business and industry, not governments, control our free market economy. Owing to the avarice of managements and the aspirations of workers, they have an in-built tendency to become uncompetitive. They should have avoided the recession by cutting pay and prices. Lending to business and industry is now regarded as volatile and bankers often favour safer mortgage loans. That is an undesirable state of affairs.

What has unilateral monetary theory, particularly monetarism, to do with any of these economic problems? What indeed? Personally, I do not think that there has been a single monetary policy since the inadequate wage freeze which has had any bearing on them. Business and industry have simply gone their own way and done whatever they pleased.

4

International Transactions

Settlement of international trade

Every country has its own basic money supply and most have their
own currencies It is necessary, therefore, to know how international
trade is settled.

Foreign parties can own or owe parts of our basic money supply
and British parties can own or owe parts of the basic money supplies
of other nations. That is the position from our point of view and the
wider one is that parties of any country can own or owe parts of the
basic money supplies of any other country.

Settlement of international transactions in sterling, where one of
the parties is British, results in the foreign-owned part of our basic
money supply being increased, reduced or left unchanged in amount
in accordance with the status rules and, of course, the constituent
parts are altered in each case. As well as owning part of our supply
(BMSC), foreign parties can incur debts on spending (BMSD).
Consequently, transactions solely in sterling between foreign parties
also affect our basic money supply in accordance with the status
rules.

A transaction, or any part of it, can only be settled in an agreed
currency. A choice has to be made. The parties may agree to
settlement in either of their currencies or in a third. Thus, a

transaction between a German party and a Spanish one could be settled in deutschmarks, pesetas or, say, pounds.

In tabular form the position would then be as follows:

Payer	*Recipient*	*Currency chosen*	*Affected basic money supply*
German	Spanish	Deutschmarks	German
German	Spanish	Pesetas	Spanish
German	Spanish	Pounds	British

Whichever the choice, BMSC and BMSD of the affected basic money supply would be equal both before and after the transaction.

British banks open and maintain foreign currency accounts with banks abroad ('correspondents') or with their own branches or subsidiary banks overseas. In like manner, foreign banks open and maintain sterling accounts in Britain with our banks or with their own branches or subsidiary banks here.

Full understanding of the effects of international trade and the settlement procedures can only be acquired through knowledge of bilateral monetary theory, banking practice and book-keeping. To this end, the use of cash and the transfer of funds by cheque or other order needs to be considered.

The carrying of cash abroad either in sterling or foreign currency has no effect on basic money supply, as it is the act of spending which matters. Foreign banks return sterling cash to this country and have it credited to their accounts here; foreign currency spent here and taken to British banks is credited to their accounts in the relevant countries – deutschmarks, for example, being paid into accounts in Germany. Thus, worldwide, cash generally follows its usual pattern; it is issued, used to settle a transaction and returned to its own banking system.

Cheques follow that pattern with identical effects, and other means of settlement, such as electronic payments, achieve the same results. The transactions are generated outside the banking systems and settled within them.

Distinction has to be made between trade transactions and those of a purely financial nature. The latter are gambling transactions in currencies and can often be financed by borrowing. It is not practicable, however, to obtain more and more borrowing to finance recurring trade deficits.

Settlement of our trade deficits is made, therefore, (1) by British debtors paying from foreign currency holdings and selling overseas assets or (2) by the foreign creditors accepting payment in sterling to an account in London, where the balances, if not overdrawn, earn interest. Such sterling is often used by the creditors to purchase assets in Britain and for setting up foreign-owned companies here. These practices may appear to be beneficial, but they are not in our longer term interests.

Foreign currency speculators or dealers running positions may, after a fall in the exchange rate of a currency, expect there will come a time when it will rebound and may gamble on this view becoming fact. The existence of the foregoing practices of foreign creditors shows just how dangerous this expectation can be.

It is estimated that about 80 per cent of the foreign exchange transactions taking place in London are unrelated to trade. Many take place between foreign holders of sterling with creditor balances. Thus, for each of the parties moving out of sterling, another moves in. Its quantity is unaffected.

Although the status rules apply to all international transactions, the general effect is that the amount of sterling available for lending overnight in the London Money Market is fairly constant.

Can basic money be imported and exported?

People are often very careless in speech. Thus, a man, having bought a house, might say that he obtained a mortgage. In fact, he obtained a loan and granted a mortgage.

In the same way, we talk of money flowing into and out of the country, of funds being attracted to, or withdrawn from, financial centres such as London, New York and Tokyo and, as an example of even more vague statements, of funds 'sloshing around the system'.

Perhaps these kinds of comment alone should have warned us

that we did not really know what we were talking about and should have revealed the need for an investigation into what happens to basic money and basic money supply. Let us try to remedy the situation.

We begin with the bare facts. People trade, and have always traded, in services, whether productive or otherwise. They earn credits (BMSC) which entitle them to purchase the services of others, and incur debts (BMSD) which they redeem by the performance of reciprocal services.

Sometimes it is said that it would be a good thing if there were only one currency in the world. Actually there is, and that currency is services. It is the means of measurement – the units of account (pounds, dollars, yen etc.) – which vary from country to country.

When international trade was settled in gold, debtors paid their accounts by transferring quantities of the metal. Gold was a medium of exchange, but it had no allegiance to any banking system. In other words, it was an international, as well as a home, medium of exchange.

It is natural, therefore, to assume that it transferred basic money from country to country. Further consideration, however, proves this view to be incorrect.

International transactions settled in gold, wherever they took place, conformed to the status rules. Accordingly, they affected the local basic money supply at the point of delivery. Payments were due in currencies and gold of the equivalent values was handed over in settlement. The basic money supply affected was the one to which the currency belonged.

As an aid to settlement, gold can never be anything more than a medium of exchange and is always nominal money. Its movements across borders did not result in the import or export of basic money.

Consider a transaction between an American exporter and a British importer. Settlement could be required in New York or London. If the gold were delivered to New York, the American basic money supply would be affected, whereas if payment had to be made in London, it is the British one which would change. Assuming the statuses of the parties were both nil, the first case would result in the exporter and the importer becoming respectively a service creditor and a service debtor in dollars in America and the second would cause them to have the same statuses in sterling in Britain. The service debtor made payment with borrowed gold; he is still in debt in terms of services and can only clear it by performing reciprocal ones or from unearned income.

The main need of service debtors is to be able to sell goods and services to others, which, in the circumstances under discussion, meant the holders of owned or borrowed gold.

Consequently, when countries lost gold through trade, their peoples had to work harder and/or charge less for their goods and services to get some back. The resulting import and export of gold gave the false impression that basic money also could be so treated.

Nowadays, international traders accept payment in foreign currencies and to some extent retain, rather than convert, them to home currencies. Large parts of the resulting balances are held by the banks in accounts in their own names, while separate ledgers, or computer records, are maintained to show the real ownership. In other words, the banks hold most of the balances to the order of their customers and the rest on their own account.

A bank in one country with no foreign currency can make a 'back-to-back' arrangement with a bank in another. Thus, if a British bank wished to acquire dollars, while an American one wanted pounds, entries could be raised so that a quantity of dollars would appear in an account in the name of the British bank in the books of the American one, while the equivalent in pounds would be credited to an account in the name of the American bank in the books of the British one.

Both banks would put cross entries through their books – a credit to an account in the name of the other bank and a debit to an account in its own name. The basic money supply in both countries would be unaffected.

We have noted that transactions can only be carried out in one currency. The basic money supply in the relevant country is affected, but it is also necessary for an equivalent cross entry to be passed through the books of a bank in the other country.

Basic money is *not* created by such a cross entry, as no performance of services is involved. The entries are simply required by the book-keeping systems. Trading transactions are the catalysts which affect the wealth and standing of the parties concerned.

No means of settlement results in basic money being imported or exported. Under currency settlements, the position from our point of view is as follows:

(a) At home, an adverse balance of trade results in more of our basic money supply credits being owned by foreign parties and in a reduction in their basic money supply debts; a favourable balance of trade results in less of our basic money supply credits being owned by foreigners and an increase in their basic money supply debts.

(b) Abroad, an adverse balance of trade results in a reduction in our foreign currency balances (BMSC) and an increase in our foreign currency debts (BMSD); a favourable balance of trade results in an increase in our foreign currency balances and a reduction in our foreign currency debts.

Service debtors borrow the deposits of service creditors, via the banks, to finance the production of goods and the supply of services. If an adverse balance of payments caused an outflow of basic money supply, there would be less funds available for lending; all the disadvantages associated with a recession would then follow. In fact, basic money supply remains in its own country and service debtors borrow deposits belonging to both home and foreign holders of creditor balances. Thus, the level of trading can be maintained.

A country can run a trading deficit as long as its currency is acceptable in settlement. When its suppliers are not prepared to accept its currency, it has to purchase or borrow foreign ones and, in these circumstances, the rates of exchange become progressively unfavourable. That is the nature of the difficulty and not an outflow of basic money supply.

We often hear of individuals transferring their financial wealth from one country to another on retirement, of international companies moving funds around the world and of criminals laundering their ill-gotten gains by switching moneys among financial centres. Again, the false impression is given that basic money can be imported or exported. Nevertheless, it cannot be done.

Before an individual or group can 'transfer funds abroad', he, she or it has to purchase the relevant foreign currency from a seller prepared to accept sterling in settlement. Thus, the sterling remains in Britain, while the purchaser becomes the owner of a quantity of foreign basic money supply credits.

Basic money can only be created by debtor spending on creditor services. Its very nature, therefore, prevents it from being imported or exported. Two questions, however, remain. (1) What is the status in a country abroad of a British purchaser of its currency seeking to transfer funds there? (2) Can a holding in one basic money supply be exchanged for a holding in another?

Originally, I took the view that to own part of another basic money supply, a service creditor must have performed services for one or more service debtors in the relevant foreign country. This is an arguable and tenable position.

Nevertheless, on further reflection, I prefer the view that a holding of basic money supply of one nation can be exchanged for an equivalent holding of another. Thus, service credits become exchangeable on an international basis. Moreover, service debts in one country can be exchanged for service debts in another.

Under the first argument, a service creditor in Britain, in having his assets realised and converted to Spanish pesetas, would retain that status and become a service debtor in Spain on spending there.

In terms of the second, such a party would relinquish the status in Britain and become a service creditor in Spain.

Bear in mind that there is a second party to each transaction and that banks act as intermediaries or on their own accounts. Assume a Spanish bank handles the transaction. It reduces its service debtor status in London by acquiring the sterling and increases its service debtor status in Spain by providing the peseta balance.

This is not a trading transaction, as the performance of services for monetary reward is not its basis. The payments are equivalent to gifts. In Britain, a service creditor has made a gift to a service debtor, thereby reducing British basic money supply; in Spain, a service debtor has made a gift to a service creditor, thereby increasing Spanish basic money supply.

From his point of view, the service creditor has succeeded in transferring his financial wealth to Spain, an imprecise and unilateral concept; in fact, he has exchanged a holding of sterling for one of pesetas. Basic money was not, therefore, exported.

Movable assets can be imported and exported, but basic money does not come into that category. The service creditor does not take an asset with him; he leaves one in Britain and acquires another in Spain. Sterling balances remain in London, dollar ones in New York and yen ones in Tokyo.

The position in relation to basic money should now be clear, but some comments on the book-keeping system are deemed appropriate. Pesetas were provided in Spain and sterling did not leave its home base. Both countries can, in consequence, support the same level of trade before and after the transactions.

Assume that, when the service creditor realises his assets in Britain, the proceeds are placed on deposit with a British bank and amount to a very considerable sum. Its office in London would make payment to the branch of the Spanish bank there. On the basis that all other things are equal in the meantime, the British bank would have to call the sum involved from the discount houses, but the Spanish bank would be able to lend it to them instead.

If the Spanish bank were fully lent at home, it would have to provide the new peseta credit at the expense of older ones, say by slowing down its lending and allowing repayments of borrowing to reduce its deposits. Thus, it would be letting payments from service creditors to service debtors reduce basic money supply to its previous level.

The book-keeping in both countries confirms that basic money has not been exported. Parties cannot *transfer* their financial wealth from one country to another; they can only *exchange* it, less charges, for an equivalent holding in another basic money supply. A contra transaction always takes place in the opposite direction.

It is sometimes said that an inflow of money causes inflation because too much money is then chasing too few goods and services. Now it can be seen that there is no inflow of basic money or basic money supply. In every country, basic money supply is only created and destroyed in accordance with the status rules.

Basic money cannot be attracted to, or withdrawn from, a financial centre, though business can; nor can it 'slosh around the system'. It follows exact rules and behaves with mathematical precision. 'Transferring', 'moving' or 'switching' are inaccurate descriptions in relation to basic money, even when it is remembered that they refer only to one side of foreign transactions; 'exchanging' is the correct description, acknowledging as it does the involvement of two parties.

Foreign investment

In general, foreign investment can take three forms:
(1) The purchase of foreign currency in the expectation that its value will increase in relation to sterling.
(2) The purchase of foreign financial securities, such as bonds, stocks and shares etc, expected to appreciate in value in relation to sterling or home investments.
(3) The buying, or setting up, of the means of production and the supply of services other than in the home country.
In all these cases the acquisition of foreign currency is necessary by purchasing, borrowing or trading.
If there were only one currency in the world, the status rules would clearly apply to the resulting 'universal' basic money supply. We already know that they apply to each individual currency in respect of domestic transactions and it is logical to assume that this must also be the case with international ones. That, however, is not good enough for our purposes, so the point must be proved.
We start by remembering that our credits and debts are in services and are measured in units of account to make them exchangeable on both the domestic and international scenes.
Parties holding matching currencies, or able to borrow them, can deal directly, when the desire to purchase coincides with the wish to sell. The basic money supply in each country is affected in accordance with the status rules. Normally, however, the services of an intermediary, such as a bank or a foreign exchange dealer, are needed in the settlement of international transactions.

(1) The purchase of foreign currency.

Four examples are worthy of consideration. They cover a wider field than simply the purchase of foreign currency in order to present a complete picture.

(a) Kevin, a service creditor in Britain, asks X Bank, which has offices in London and New York, to purchase US$ 15,000 and to hold them as an investment.

We shall assume that the exchange rate is US$1.50 to the pound; moreover, we can ignore the spread between buying and selling prices, together with exchange commission, as they are not relevant to the contentions, and use a simplified version of the book-keeping system.

In London, X Bank debits Kevin's creditor account £10,000 and credits this sum to an internal account of its own. A service creditor has made payment to a service debtor, so the basic money supply in Britain has been reduced.

In New York, X Bank credits Kevin with US$15,000 and debits an internal account of its own. A service debtor has made payment to a service creditor, so the basic money supply in the United States has been increased.

The amount of universal basic money supply is unchanged. Kevin has simply exchanged a holding in sterling for an equivalent one in dollars. If the dollars appreciate in value in relation to sterling, Kevin's gain will be matched by the bank's loss on realisation. As always, therefore, basic money supply credits equal basic money supply debts in both countries.

(b) Leslie, a service debtor in Britain, borrows £10,000 from X Bank and has this sum converted to US$15,000 to reduce his indebtedness in the United States. He believes that the dollar will appreciate in relation to sterling.

In London, X Bank debits £10,000 to Leslie's overdrawn account and credits an internal account of its own. One service debtor has made payment to another, so the basic money supply in Britain is unchanged.

In New York, a year ago, Leslie was granted a loan of US$ 50,000, which was credited to an account in his name. His present balance is US$30,000, so he owes US$20,000. The bank credits his account US$15,000, making the balance US$45,000 and reducing his debt to US$5,000. One service debtor has made payment to another, so the basic money supply in the United States is unchanged.

This is a prudent step, rather than an investment, but it allows us to note that international service debts can be exchanged as well as such service credits. The amount of universal basic money supply is unchanged.

(c) Malcolm, a service debtor in Britain, arranges through X Bank in London to borrow US$15,000 and to have this sum held as an investment.

This is a less likely scenario for an individual, but some financial organisations have been granted facilities for this type of bank borrowing. Again, I would point out that I consider this practice to be a misuse of valuable funds available for lending and would like to see it stopped. I have no objection to parties using their own or collected service credits for gambling, but not borrowed ones. Nevertheless, we have to look at the effects.

The loan could simply be made in New York by X Bank crediting Malcolm with US$15,000 and debiting an account of its own there. In that case the credit must not be mistaken for a deposit of basic money supply credits; it is simply one side of a cross entry and is part of a banking system under which overdrafts are not allowed. Basic money cannot be created by lending.

In Britain, a similar facility in sterling could be set up by a bank crediting the appropriate sum to one account and debiting it to another, both in the customer's name. Computers offset such accounts when calculating deposits and advances.

In practice, X Bank in London would debit Malcolm's account £10,000 and credit an internal account of its own. One service debtor would then have made payment to another leaving basic money supply unchanged.

In New York, X Bank would credit Malcolm's account with US$15,000 and debit an internal account of its own. A service debtor has made payment to a service creditor, so basic money has been created. This time the deposit is real and does not represent a loan.

Universal basic money supply has been increased, but Malcolm's net position is unchanged. He is more of a service debtor in Britain, but that is offset to the extent that he is a service creditor in the United States.

(d) Norman, a service creditor in Britain, asks X Bank in London to debit £10,000 to his account and have US$15,000 deducted from his loan account in New York, where the balance appears as a deposit.

In London, X Bank debits his account £10,000 and credits an internal account of its own. A service creditor has made payment to a service debtor, so the basic money supply in Britain has been reduced.

In New York, X Bank credits Norman's deposit (loan) account US$15,000 and debits an internal account of its own. One service debtor has made payment to another, so the basic money supply in the United States is unchanged.

Universal basic money supply has been reduced, but Norman's net position is unaltered. He is less of a service creditor in Britain, but that is offset to the extent that he is less of a service debtor in the United States.

No performance of services for monetary reward is involved in these four examples and they are more akin to gifts, which, of course, affect basic money in exactly the same way as trading transactions in accordance with the status rules.

Since the parties involved have a status, sometimes the same, sometimes different, in two countries, it is as if each were two parties instead of just one. Thus, Kevin in Britain made a gift to Kevin in New York.

Summing up, the effects of the dealings were as follows:

Status Britain	Status USA	British BMS	US BMS	Universal BMS
(a) Creditor	Creditor	Reduced	Increased	Unchanged
(b) Debtor	Debtor	Unchanged	Unchanged	Unchanged
(c) Debtor	Creditor	Unchanged	Increased	Increased
(d) Creditor	Debtor	Reduced	Unchanged	Reduced

The logical assumption has proved to be correct; the status rules cannot be broken and govern both domestic and international transactions.

The effect of the transactions, however, does not rest there. In the normal course of events, British and American banks are fully lent. Consequently, the transactions, whether involving credits or debits, have to be accommodated, where necessary, at the expense of existing balances. As we might have expected, therefore, universal basic money supply would be unchanged in total.

(2) The purchase of foreign financial securities.

If the purpose in acquiring foreign currency is to invest in such securities, the subsequent transactions become domestic ones in the relevant countries and comply with the status rules. Thus, the items concerned are forms of debt and dealings in them change the constituent parts of basic money supply in line with the direct investment status rules.

(3) The buying, or setting up, of the means of production or the supply of services.

In many cases, the acquisition of foreign currency is the result of parties accepting it in settlement of trade debts. Instead of exchanging the currency for the home one, it can be used for the aforementioned purposes. The subsequent transactions are domestic ones in the countries concerned and conform to the status rules.

Reserve currencies

Sometimes a currency is used both inside and outside its home area for the settlement of transactions between foreigners. The currency is then said to be a reserve one.

For example, United States dollars spent in Russia are often retained there by the recipients and used instead of roubles to settle local transactions. This practice creates and destroys American basic money supply, not Russian, in accordance with the status rules.

The dollars were originally purchased in the United States by

the spenders and the relevant funds were used to purchase government debt. Consequently, while they remain in circulation, the
United States Treasury is gaining the benefit of an interest-free
loan.

It should be remembered that banknotes are vouchers for general
purchases in the same way as a luncheon voucher is for a specific
one.

Exchange rates

Fixed and floating exchange rates, devaluations and our temporary
membership of the Exchange Rate Mechanism have failed to cure
our recurring balance of payments deficits and to eliminate inflation.
This is hardly surprising, as an exchange rate is not a catalyst of any
kind; it is, when not fixed, a mirror image of what has happened in
the market-place. In other words, that reflection is mathematically
precise.

Thus, if all other things are equal in the meantime, an adverse
balance in our terms of trade would result in falling sterling
exchange rates. Though weak in trend, they have held up better than
might have been expected. This, however, has been due to foreign
creditors accepting payment for our imports in sterling; the funds
acquired have been used to strengthen their positions in the City of
London, to invest in our companies, to buy our property and to build
factories in our country. True to form, the exchange rates have
reflected the events.

Interest rates are sometimes raised in the belief that this action will
encourage foreign holders not to sell sterling. Experience has shown
that this practice is futile for its purpose and damaging to the
economy.

Speculation against sterling takes place from time to time. A
correct defence would be to use foreign currency holdings to buy our
cheapening currency and then suddenly to cut pay and prices.
Sterling would appreciate in value and more foreign currency than
held before could be purchased. A large profit would be made and no
party would ever again readily speculate against sterling.

That, of course, is an extreme example, but it is equally true that few parties would speculate against a currency, the value of which is subject to control by pay and price adjustments.

Contrary to unilateral monetary theory, pay and prices are the only effective levers in the management of an economy and the protection of a currency's value.

European Monetary Union

Much has been said and written recently in favour of, or against, monetary union. The media seem to have reduced the argument to a dispute between those who want to be good Europeans and the rest, who wish to retain sovereignty over our economic affairs. All the debating has gone on without any knowledge of bilateral monetary theory, so it is little wonder that no clear-cut case, either way, has been made. Let us take advantage of our new knowledge to resolve the issue logically.

A free trading area improves the level of business and benefits all participants, but monetary union is a very different matter. We must, therefore, look closely at its prospective effects.

A currency has to have a home. In illustration, the banking systems in Britain and the United States of America transfer the surplus local funds to London and New York respectively; these funds form part of the sterling balances in the first-named city and the dollar ones in the second; such balances do not leave their home countries.

In Britain, the main service debtors, the corporate ones, come to London to discuss and obtain their borrowing requirements. Most of the major lending is agreed in that city, though sometimes with the approval of a bank head office elsewhere. In London, any funds not utilised are lent overnight to the discount houses, a practice which shows how efficient the system has become. Thus, full use is made of the funds available for lending.

What would happen if we gave up our currency and accepted the proposed euro in a monetary union? Our sterling balances, having been converted to euros, would begin to leave the country.

Where would they go? The answer, at present, is Frankfurt-am-Main. The European Monetary Institute, which is intended to become the European central bank, has already been sited there. In effect, the euro would become a deutschmark in everything but name. Germany would retain sovereignty, while all the other member states gave theirs up.

Surplus local deposits from all over the countries in the European Union would be transferred to Frankfurt. The main service debtors would still come initially to London for their borrowing requirements, but, given our recurring trade deficits, British banks would not own or control enough euros to meet them. The ultimate decisions in many cases would rest with German bankers, requiring visits to Frankfurt which might well prove fruitless. The fates of British banking, business and industry would lie in German hands.

All major financial institutions, such as European banks, insurance companies and discount houses, would have to be represented in Frankfurt. The flight of euros would, therefore, be followed by a transfer of people and jobs to that city. Britain, and her other partners, could find that they had become minor provinces in a German financial empire. None, however, stands to lose as much as we do. Incidentally, the Germans might not welcome the influx of so many – er – Europeans.

At some stage the Germans might move the financial centre from Frankfurt to Berlin, which, in effect, would make the latter city the capital of Europe. Nevertheless, the objection is not to a German city: it is to the movement of balances, people and jobs, together with the impoverishment of the areas they would leave behind.

The interests of the countries at the centre of the common market are not the same as those on the fringes. Germany would gain from monetary union and to a much lesser extent so might France and the Benelux countries, though the high price would be the loss of considerable control over their affairs. The other countries – not just Britain – need to retain their currencies for their own protection. It is simply not desirable that the centre should attract balances, people, jobs and, inevitably, power; the need is to spread the benefits outwards from the centre and not solely in the form of hand-outs.

The bureaucrats are obsessed with harmonisation, whereas only competition can give continuing life to the European Union. In any event, how does one harmonise geography?

Countries joining the European Union expect to make some concessions, but to have their major interests looked after and strengthened. London, New York and Tokyo are the three main financial centres in the world and invisible earnings are very important to Britain.

Our membership, with the help of our partners, should have been of great benefit to our financial centre and the European Monetary Institute should have been sited in London. Germany has the industry; Britain needs the financial aspects. As events transpired, Germany insisted on the European Monetary Institute being established in Frankfurt-am-Main; moreover, when sterling got into difficulties in the Exchange Rate Mechanism, Germany declined to support it. One might say that these actions were a declaration of financial 'war'.

We are entirely to blame for our economic weakness, but the Germans, instead of acting like good Europeans, chose not only to put their own interests first, but to gain at our expense. They are now pressing for monetary union on the same basis.

The financial war has followed the same pattern as the military one. The Benelux countries have been overrun, France has surrendered and Italy is a half-hearted ally. In these circumstances, Britain can never be at the heart of Europe and we need to seek allies to oppose too much power being concentrated in the centre. After all, the balance of power was the policy which served our nation so well over centuries of history. In Europe, nothing changes.

Our partners should recognise that Britain has many more commitments to the outside world than they do. We have, therefore, to remain an international trading nation and must learn to compete with the stronger ones, such as Japan. We can only do this if we retain control of our currency and economic affairs. The case might be different if Europe were doing better than Japan and the 'tiger' economies.

Unfortunately, monetary union is being allowed to develop a momentum of its own. If then we wish the European Union to be a partnership of sovereign states, we must oppose it now and reject a wait-and-see policy. Otherwise, it is probable that monetary union will take place in the centre – Germany, France and the Benelux countries – in spite of objections from outside. At best, monetary union should be abandoned; at worst, sterling should be retained as an alternative and competing currency to the German euro for the settlement of European and international transactions.

If monetary union is introduced, it is desirable that it should be in part rather than whole, so that the effects can be studied on the smaller scale before too much damage is done. Would the French welcome the disappearance of their currency and the movement of their franc balances, converted to euros, from Paris to Frankfurt-am-Main? Somehow, I think they would soon be clamouring to reverse any decision adopting the single currency.

The economy is a local issue, not a central one. It is simply the sum total of local activities. In general, people live, work and spend in local areas and, when obliged to move, put down roots on a similar basis elsewhere. Every local area, whether in the same monetary area or not, has to compete with the rest of the world for its share of business.

Accordingly, there is actually a case for saying that outlying areas, like Scotland and Northern Ireland, should have their own currencies. In other respects, such as defence, it is desirable to maintain a common front.

Summing up, monetary union is unnecessary, undesirable and divisive. The best solution would be for those advocating it to stop so doing. The probability is that any nation giving up its currency will live to regret that decision.

There are two sides to every argument and I would like to have been able to list some of the points of consequence in favour of the good Europeans. Unfortunately, in the light of the dangers we face, I cannot find any practical ones. Indeed, I believe that only subservience and further humiliation are on offer.

5

Reality versus False Monetary Theory

'Money'

In this chapter, when false theories are being discussed, 'money' is used in accordance with normal practice. Thus, it can refer to basic money (credits and debts in services), nominal money (media of exchange and bank deposits), purchasing power or the unit of account (the pound). Readers should now have no difficulty in realising which interpretation should be put on the term.

One view is that it is all right to define 'money' in any way one chooses, provided that the use is consistent. I regard this opinion as woolly-minded and it is the very antithesis of my own contentions. Definitions must be as precise as one can make them.

The basis of false concepts

Unilateral monetary theory is a compilation of opinions built up over the centuries. Unfortunately, they are based on a view of the nature of money which is logically untenable. The result is that virtually the whole subject is unsound. I know that this is a remarkable thing to have to say. The truth, however, is that owing to the accuracy of the monetary, banking and settlement systems, the economy is mathematically precise and we get exactly the state of affairs our collective behaviour warrants. We are not, therefore, at the mercy of a monetary phenomenon and can improve the performance of the economy by changing our behaviour to favour such an outcome.

The obsession with false monetary theory, particularly monetarism, has prevented us from correctly diagnosing our economic problems. For example, a false view in vogue is that money, once created, has to be held and can have a velocity of circulation in excess of one; moreover, its supply is wrongly regarded as a stock, which can be increased or decreased by open market operations. Thus, the buying of government securities by the state from the public is deemed to increase the money supply, while the selling of such items to the public is thought to have the opposite effect.

In contrast, we know that basic money is subject to a process of continuous creation and destruction, that it can only be used once, that its supply is better described as a flow and that financial dealings have limited effects.

Every notion based on the misconceptions, no matter how eminent its proponent, past or present, is inevitably unsound. Surprising perhaps, but unavoidable without proper and precise definitions of basic and nominal money.

From the time the false concepts were accepted, the economics profession has moved steadily further from the true position. So much so that, in my experience, it is very difficult to get anyone in authority or academic circles to consider any contentions which are not based on the establishment's misconceptions and do not have equally suspect bibliographies in support.

With the truth about basic and nominal money now known, we can look at some anomalies apparent in the teaching and show how they arise from misconceptions. Then, we can turn our attention to some of the major false theories and related issues. In this connection, we have to bear in mind that cash and bank deposits are regarded as money by the authorities and are included in their definitions of the money supply, numbered from M1 to M5.

Anomalies

Example 1

Assume that a bank's depositors withdraw a sum equal to the total of its cash, Bank of England balance, money at call and immediately realisable investments and that it makes up its balance sheet at this point. An amount would appear against Deposits, but there would be no cash. The bank could not cash another cheque nor pay one presented specially or through the clearing system even though drawn on a creditor account. So, if deposits are purchasing power, where has that of the remaining ones gone?

This is a situation which could arise, but is unlikely to do so in respect of a competent bank. Depositors leave their funds in their accounts to meet commitments and for safe custody, so, unless confidence has been shaken, have no reason to change their behaviour. The issue, nevertheless, is important, because, although purchasing power was deposited, it has not all been retained.

At the time they are paid in, deposits are basic money supply credits. Most of these funds are borrowed by the custodians and then lent, leaving the accounts simply as records of ownership. In the face of a run, a bank can pay out its cash, Bank of England balance, money at call and the value of its immediately realisable investments. The Bank of England or another deposit-taker could lend it funds to meet further demand, but these would not come from the stricken bank's own deposits.

Statements show the transactions which have passed through accounts and the resulting balances are the sums the bank is responsible for (deposits) or is owed (advances). The purchasing power of the depositors is dependent on the ability of the bank to meet their cheques and withdrawals and not on the balances of their accounts. Thus, in the example, the bank could pay out the items mentioned and no more from its own resources. Deposits are records and not basic money or purchasing power.

Example 2

Imagine that three persons, A, B and C, make up a community and have a total nominal money supply of three £1 notes, which are presently owned by A. They have no bank deposits. A asks B to look after his £3 and B lends £2 to C. It is obvious that the supply is still £3, yet B is now acting as a banker and could produce a balance sheet showing Deposits £3, Overdrafts £2 and Cash £1. If notes and deposits are counted, the supply becomes £6. Thus, if B makes out a balance sheet, the supply is £6 and, if he does not, it is £3. Presumably no one would argue that the supply had been increased, if C had borrowed £2 directly from A, yet where is the difference in C borrowing directly or indirectly from A? Do we really believe that B can alter the position by writing up a set of books?

This is an example of the confusion of cash and deposits with basic money. We could assume that A is a service creditor for £3 and that B and C must be service debtors in total for that amount. Are we jumping to a false conclusion? Could A be a service creditor to a greater extent? Suppose the circumstances are as follows.

B works for A and, in return, receives food, clothing and shelter; C is a manufacturer and four weeks ago undertook to supply goods to A for £15. During that time, he has borrowed £3 per week from A and used the cash to buy necessities from him. Thus, he owes A £12 and the breakdown of the basic money supply in respect of these transactions is:

$$\text{A BMSC £12} \qquad \text{C BMSD £12}$$

A deposits the three £1 notes with B, thereby obliging C to borrow from B instead. C decides he only needs £2 this week for his purchases from A, but has not yet carried out this transaction. BMSC and BMSD remain at £12.

There is, therefore, no necessary relationship between, on the one hand, cash and deposits and, on the other, basic money or basic money supply. B cannot alter the position by writing up a set of books.

Example 3
Company A has a creditor balance, while Company B has a debtor one. If the former pays a debt to the latter by cheque, the money supply falls, because deposits are down, but if the payment is made in the opposite direction, the money supply rises, because deposits

are up. Thus, similar actions have contrary results. Yet if money
were a stock, payments between parties should leave it unchanged in
amount.

We, of course, now know that Company A's creditor spending
on Company B's debtor services would reduce the basic money
supply, while Company B's debtor spending on Company A's
creditor services would increase it. The book-keeping represents
the facts.

There is always an outstanding amount of basic money supply, but
it is ever-changing and never made up of the same constituents. It is
comparable to a queue of lemmings preparing to throw themselves
over a cliff into the sea; they do not come back out of the sea. A flow
of lemmings, yes – a stock, no.

Each part of the basic money supply created and each part
destroyed relates to a specific service. The same transaction cannot
be repeated, though a similar one can be carried out. Like a lemming
going over a cliff, a service cannot come back for a repeat performance. Basic money, as we know from experience, can only be
spent once. Cash can be reused, but the transactions it settles are
separate. Basic money supply is better described as a flow than a
stock.

Example 4
We are told that cash is money, but luncheon vouchers are not. Yet,
the vouchers perform a function which would otherwise require the
use of cash. How then can we accept this contention? A tax
concession is, of course, involved, but that is not a material issue in
regard to the point in question.

Both cash and luncheon vouchers are nominal, and not basic,
money.

The anomalies in the four examples have now been dealt with.
They are not really anomalies at all; it is the teaching which is
wrong. Once it is corrected, the anomalies disappear.

The Theory of the Pyramid of Credit

This theory is based on a reasoning process running on the following lines:

A bank is operating on a liquidity ratio of, say, 30 per cent; A deposits £300; B borrows £210 from the bank and uses this sum to buy raw materials from C; C deposits £210 with the bank and so on. Thus, with an original deposit of £300, the bank can in theory produce figures in relation to it as follows:

Deposits	£1,000	Overdrafts	£700
		Cash	300
			£1,000

The contention is that the bank has created credit, and hence money (purchasing power), to the extent of the additional deposits.

Borrowers do not obtain funds without purpose and the banks require sound reasons and full expectations of repayment before they will lend. Why then did B borrow? If he is a manufacturer, he would have reason to believe that he could sell his products. He would look upon depositors like A as potential customers. He may even have an order from A.

Let us assume that this is the case, that he borrows £210 from the bank to purchase raw materials from C and that he has undertaken to manufacture some goods for A at a price of £231, allowing £21 as profit for himself. A no longer has uncommitted purchasing power of £300. £231 of his balance is effectively frozen, so that the lending, far from increasing purchasing power from £300 to £510 (being A's £300 plus C's £210), appears to have reduced it to £279 (being the uncommitted part of A's balance plus C's £210).

To obtain a clear comparison, assume firstly that A pays B in advance. The bank's figures would then be:

(1)	Deposits	A	£ 69	Cash	£300
		B	21		
		C	210		
			£300		

If B borrows from the bank, the figures are:

(2) Deposits	A	£300	Advances	B	£210
	C	210	Cash		300
		£510			£510

In the first situation, A, B and C clearly have uncommitted purchasing power totalling £300.

In the second, A and C appear to have total purchasing power of £510, but A's commitment reduces this to £279. Where has the difference of £21 gone? The answer is that B is in a position to obtain £21 of credit. He expects to receive £231 from A and he owes the bank £210. Therefore, he can run up debts of £21.

The conclusions are that each party has exactly the same amount of purchasing power in both cases, that the bank's lending has not increased it and that, in the given circumstances, it always equals the cash held by the bank.

When B buys raw materials from C, he becomes a service debtor spending on creditor services. Basic money is created by that action. C's deposit of £210 reflects the rise in trading activity and does not represent competing funds of an inflationary nature created out of thin air. Basic money supply can only be created by the performance of services and there is no way in which basic money supply credits can become different in total from basic money supply debts. The creation of basic money by lending, bank or otherwise, is impossible.

Deposits rose by 70 per cent when B borrowed from the bank and bought raw materials from C. Again, we must maintain our perspective. In normal circumstances, thousands of transactions are taking place and deposits, like the basic money supply, would only increase or fall slightly on balance at any one time in relation to their total amount.

The monetary and banking systems are highly beneficial and increase the capacity of the community to trade. That is what builds up deposits and advances and not the mythical pyramid of credit. In the argument supporting the false concept, the service debtors only borrow; they do not perform reciprocal services! These would reduce basic money supply and show up as payments from depositors to borrowers. Put another way, the depositors only save and do not spend. Where does the economics profession find these obliging parties?

Assume that A is a bank's first customer and deposits £100, £70 of which it lends to B. It is obvious that B now holds 70 per cent of A's funds. If then banks used single-entry book-keeping systems, outgoings would be deducted from incomings and the true position would be clear. The remaining balance – the cash holding – would be seen to be the net result of the transactions and not a base for a pyramid of credit.

Titles to basic money simply flow through the hands of banks. The incoming funds consist of deposits and loan repayments, while the outgoing ones are made up of depositors' withdrawals and loans. Eight per cent of deposits is always retained, thereby giving the impression that banks can create credit, and hence money, to the extent of 12 $\frac{1}{2}$ times their cash holdings.

Lending is not an invention of the banks. Would-be borrowers formerly approached the holders of funds directly and no one claimed that this procedure created money. Now they have access to the same funds, deposits, via the banks. In principle, nothing has changed.

As we noted earlier in the discussion on the goldsmith, he could have kept his stock in such a way that gold received was stacked at the back, while that paid out was taken from the front. The theoretical idea of a flow of gold then becomes fact, while the notion of a pyramid of credit built on a cash base is shown to be a fantasy.

Credit creation theory

The examples which support credit creation theory take many forms and, since it is necessary to eliminate any doubts, some more are presented together with the reasons for rejecting them. The false theory is not simply to be questioned; it must be eradicated completely.

In one example, a customer asks his bank for a loan and offers government debt in security. The latter is a claim on the government and the bank exchanges it for a claim on itself, which it is contended can be used as purchasing power. In illustration, assume that Mr Jones, a manufacturer, asks his bank for a loan of £5,000, that he offers in security £10,000 8 per cent Treasury Stock 2009 and that the bank duly grants him overdraft facilities to the extent requested.

The argument then runs that the creation of credit takes place when he uses these facilities to purchase goods and services from others. Thus, assuming Mr Jones issues cheques totalling £5,000 and that the payees have creditor accounts into which they pay the cheques, bank deposits will increase by this sum. Such deposits, it is claimed, are money (purchasing power) and the bank has, therefore, created an additional £5,000.

Many holders of investments would be service creditors, so most of the argument can be rejected on those grounds alone. Assume, however, that Mr Jones is a service debtor.

As the bank does not lend its own funds, the claim is on deposits, already on hand. There is, therefore, no net creation of money (purchasing power) by the bank.

Considering the matter further, if the contention were correct, a bank would be able to start up business with a loan as its first transaction. Assume that Mr Jones is X Bank's first customer and that it grants him overdraft facilities of up to £5,000. He writes a cheque for this amount in favour of Mr Brown and the latter pays it into his creditor account with Y Bank, which in turn presents it to X Bank for payment. Since X Bank has no deposits and banks do not use their own capital for lending, it cannot pay the cheque. It has, therefore, been unable to create basic money.

Assume that X Bank's second customer is Mr Smith and that he deposits £5,000 in cash before the cheque drawn by Mr Jones is presented. X Bank is now able to pay the cheque on presentation. Again, no new funds have been created. All that has happened is that the purchasing power given up by Mr Smith has been transferred to Mr Brown's bank. Mr Smith still has a deposit of £5,000, but let him try to draw it out. He would find that X Bank could not repay it. Equally, if he issued a cheque, it could not be paid on presentation.

As Mr Jones is a service debtor, basic money supply credits are increased by his spending. The suppliers of goods and services, however, are usually service debtors also, so it is rather unlikely that, if he used the facilities to the full, £5,000 would be paid to service creditors. Assuming average conditions, basic money supply would only increase moderately on balance. It is Mr Jones who increases basic money supply debts by spending, and not the bank by lending.

No doubt Mr Jones intends to repay his borrowing by performing services in his own field, but is unable to do so immediately. When his cheques are presented, the bank has to meet them in his stead.

It should be noted that any creation of basic money took place as Mr Jones issued his cheques. Thus, it happened before the lending and not the other way round.

The example comes close to the true process in stating that 'the creation of money takes place when he uses these facilities to purchase goods and services from others'. It soon goes off the rails, however, and ends with the false conclusion that the bank has created an additional £5,000.

When service creditor payees of the cheques issued by Mr Jones deposit them, that action is a redisposition of the basic money created. The bank receives the basic money supply credits, though they were not created by lending, and amends its records, deposits, to show that it has. Basic money, remember, is intangible, as it is services in which we trade. Media of exchange are needed to move it.

The example touches on the process by which basic money is created – debtor spending on creditor services – but we must not forget that the other process which destroys basic money – creditor spending on debtor services – is going on at the same time. In a fully reasoned argument, the two cannot be separated; otherwise, we could devise an example which 'proves' that more basic money is being destroyed than has been created!

An example which deceives many people is the following one:

Andrew has £2,000. He uses this sum to buy marketable securities and asks his bank manager to let him have a loan of £1,500 against the pledging of these items. When the loan is agreed, he invests this amount and is fortunate enough to see his investments increase in value to, say, £7,000. Again, he approaches his bank manager and asks for his loan to be increased from £1,500 to £5,000 on pledging the further securities in support. He invests the additional £3,500 and so on. The contention is that money is being created by this process and can be realised by the sale of the securities.

This argument is unsound as it takes only Andrew's side of the transactions into account and ignores the involvement of other parties. It can, therefore, can be defeated on its own grounds.

In any event, we can dismiss it out of hand for we know that banks cannot create basic money by lending. The effects of financial dealings such as those described are set out on pages 76 to 77 and are confirmed by the basic money supply accounting formula.

Another example claims that banks can create money by making investments. Thus, X Bank buys securities from Z plc, one of its large customers, for £10 million and in settlement pays this sum into the company's creditor account. The contention is that X Bank has thereby created £10 million of purchasing power.

Again, this argument can be readily dismissed, since it is just another example of financial dealings in shares. A further point of interest is that Z plc is probably a service debtor in spite of the creditor account. It has borrowed its capital from the public and spent itself into debt in terms of services; on the one hand, it may have performed services of greater value and become a service creditor or, on the other, it may have several accounts, with its borrowings exceeding its deposits. Most major companies operate within the limits of their borrowing facilities. Even if Z plc became a service creditor, it would lose this status on payment of its dividend. A payment of that type has the same effect as a gift. In the case of Z plc, it would be made partly as a service creditor and partly as a service debtor. There would, of course, be no effect on the basic money supply if a major service creditor were the seller of the securities.

A further example favouring credit creation runs on the following lines. The banks buy some Treasury Bills issued by the Exchequer for borrowing purposes. When the proceeds are spent, the cash returns to the banks via their depositors. Deposits (liabilities) and cash (liquid assets) increase. The banks will now be able to supply more credit, since only a proportion of deposits needs to be covered by liquid assets. Consequently, a gain of liquid assets can have a disproportionately greater effect on the availability of bank credit.

For instance, a bank is operating on a liquidity ratio of 30 per cent thus, for every £30 of cash received, it can increase its lending by £70. The lower the liquidity ratio is, the higher are the possible increases in credit. Our commercial banks operate on a cash ratio of 8 per cent and, on that basis, it is contended that credit can be increased by $12^{1}/_{2}$ times a cash gain. Yes, in spite of the different wording, we are back to the Theory of the Pyramid of Credit.

When the banks buy Treasury Bills, or other government securities it is because they have surplus funds which they would prefer to lend. They would still be unable to lend funds on the return of the funds via the depositors. The supply of credit measured by the demand would be unaffected.

The surplus funds show up in the accounts maintained by the banks with the Bank of England and are part of the liquid assets. The Treasury Bills would be paid for with bankers' payments drawn on these accounts. When the funds came back to the banks via the depositors, they would restore the Bank of England balances and, in consequence, the surpluses also. On this basis, the banks could go on buying Treasury Bills *ad infinitum*. Why does the rate of interest on them not fall to derisory levels?

Let us revert to reality. Far from there being a major upsurge in deposits, any increase would be marginal and of little account. The suppliers of goods and services are usually bank borrowers. When, therefore, the Exchequer borrows and spends, most of the funds go into debtor accounts. Thus, the Exchequer borrowing mainly replaces other borrowing; bank investments rise and advances fall.

When the banks, service debtors, purchase Treasury Bills issued by the Exchequer, another service debtor, no change takes place in basic money supply. Spending by the Exchequer on creditor services and financial payments for, say, social security to service creditors create basic money. Resulting deposits are a correct reflection of an increase in the purchasing power of the community and are not a multiple of liquid assets received.

Maintain the perspective and remember that the state has continuous income from taxes and fees. Payments from service creditors to the Exchequer destroy basic money.

Where are all the borrowers supposed to come from to support a pyramid of credit? Is it believed that when a customer asks for a loan his name goes on a waiting list pending the next purchase of Treasury Bills? Do we think that, when a public house obtains more beer, a flood of new customers descends upon it? Why then is it imagined that the equivalent can happen with bank credit?

Owing to the false teaching, governments all over the world believe that they can control the basic money supply by open market operations. Thus, they think that buying government securities increases the basic money supply and stimulates the economy, while selling them has the reverse effects. Yet, the truth is that such financial dealings have little net effect on basic money supply and, in any event, are undesirable.

Why then do the authorities go wrong? In the first place, they do not have a proper definition of money and believe that it is a single item and, in the second, it would appear that they do not fully understand the banking systems.

On the second count, the economy can be divided into two sectors, private and state. Transactions, on a daily basis, causing a net inflow of funds to the private sector from the state one create surpluses in the London money market, while those causing a net outflow result in shortages; transactions between parties in the same sector have no effect on the funds available for lending overnight in the money market.

A service debtor customer of Bank A borrows £10 million and spends it on the creditor services of a customer of Bank B. Basic money has been created. Bank B presents the cheque to Bank A and the latter gives the former a banker's payment drawn on its Bank of England account. Advances and deposits both rise, reflecting the increase in the basic money supply.

There are, however, no extra funds for lending overnight to the discount houses, this lending being part of the banks' liquidity ratios. Thus, if all other things are equal in the meantime, Bank A has to call £10 million from the discount houses and Bank B is able to lend them the funds instead.

In an attempt to reduce the basic money supply, the Bank of England sells government securities to the private sector. *Ceteris paribus*, the transactions create a shortage in the money market. The banks call the funds from the discount houses, which sell government securities to the Bank of England, thereby negating the effects of the original sales. Those effects, however, did not involve the creation and destruction of basic money.

The principle is simple. In the mopping up of surpluses and the relieving of shortages, cash flows in one direction and government securities in the other.

The Bank of England has in the past taken Special Deposits from the banks to reduce the basic money supply. Again, *ceteris paribus*, the transactions created shortages in the money market. The Bank then negated the effects of the Special Deposits by relieving the shortages.

Assess these actions against the true situation. Basic money can only be created and destroyed by trading transactions. Borrowings do not affect it nor do redispositions such as Special Deposits.

Bank deposits are sometimes classified as active and passive. The basis of the distinction is that in regard to active deposits the bank takes the first step, whereas in regard to passive ones a customer is the catalyst. Thus, deposits deemed to have resulted from a bank's purchase of securities or lending activities would be described as active, but those made by a customer or transferred from another bank would be said to be passive. We have already seen that a bank cannot unilaterally increase its deposits by purchasing securities from a customer, as the latter's behaviour has also to be taken into account. The same principle would apply to any other action taken independently by a bank, so the concept of active and passive deposits is false.

In any event, it overlooks the normal banking practices. The customer is usually the initiator in transactions and the banker responds to needs and requests. In a nutshell, therefore, the relationship is normally initiator and responder. An exception arises when a banker demands repayment of an advance, but in these circumstances the relationship has hardened to the legal one of creditor and debtor.

It has been contended that a bank can also create active deposits by expenditure of its own, say, on new premises, being settled by a credit to a customer's account. The banks run at a profit. Hence, in the normal course of business, more money passes from the customers' accounts to the banks than in the other direction. The position is brought to near equilibrium when dividends are paid and profit retentions are invested, say, in government securities and property. There is, therefore, no new source of deposits from bank expenditure, but even if there were, such deposits would correctly reflect debtor spending on creditor services. It should also be borne in mind that most of the suppliers of goods and services are borrowers and bank expenditure often reduces advances.

For the purposes of their arguments, monetary theorists often divide the economy into parts. As usual in such circumstances, more and more distinctions are made. Fortunately, we do not have to go too deeply into this subject and comment can be restricted to the main parts. Leaving aside the international one, these are the private, the banking and the state parts of the internal economy. Once divisions have been accepted, it is possible to advance arguments which purport to demonstrate that within a part some funds (outside moneys) are assets, while others (inside moneys) are not. It can be noted here for the record that such arguments exist.

The converse concepts, however, are that there is only one undivided internal economy linked to all the others in the world by trade and through the banking system, that moneys (basic money) are always assets and that the experiences of us all, whether acting as individuals or in concert, are precisely the same. These are the contentions in this book.

Consider another example of credit creation theory. The bank used by two parties utilises the deposits of one to make a loan of £500 to the other. Both now have the money to spend. This practice causes too much money to chase too few goods. Consequently, inflation results.

In making the loan available, the bank has chosen to credit the relevant sum to a creditor account in the borrower's name and debit it to a debtor one similarly designated. Both deposits and advances then increased and the impression is given that money has been created. In truth, nothing has happened except that the bank has adjusted its records to suit itself. The entries offset each other. If the loan had been granted on overdraft, deposits would not have increased and advances would only rise when the funds were drawn. That is the real situation. A banker cannot create basic money with a stroke of his pen.

As a generalisation, deposits fall into three categories: (1) funds already owing in respect of bills and accruing debts not yet paid; (2) funds required for spending necessary to maintain standards of living on food, clothing, shelter, heating, etc; (3) funds which the holders have no immediate intention of spending or are deliberately saving. For ease of reference, we can name these categories, (1) Owings, (2) Commitments and (3) Savings.

In like manner, lending can be split into two groups as follows: (1) corporate finance, that is, funds borrowed on a continuing basis by suppliers in the knowledge that the indebtedness can be reduced or kept within agreed limits as goods and services are sold; (2) personal borrowing, being funds obtained by people who want to live beyond their current means and buy houses, cars, consumer durables, etc, with loans.

Now it can readily be seen that the suppliers are unable to sell goods and services to the holders of deposits in the third category. Yet if a large part of the basic money supply were allowed to go out of action, the standard of living would fall dramatically. In pursuing their own interests, banks lend or invest these dormant funds and push them back into use.

In the example, both parties are deemed to have the money to spend. The original deposit, however, falls into the second category, whereas the loan would be made from deposits in the third one. Banks do not separate deposits in this way, but that is the effect in practice.

The demands of both the depositor and the borrower have been anticipated. As a result, the goods they will buy are already in the shops at fixed prices. The buying cannot, therefore, cause too much money to chase too few goods.

Transactions between customers are settled by cross entries. Outgoing ones to non-customers result in the bank having to pay out cash or reduce its balance at the Bank of England. If both customers spend the apparently duplicated £500 with non-customers, the bank would lose £1,000. Clearly then, the bank made the loan from its reserves. It did not use the deposits of one to make a loan of £500 to the other.

Banks deal in titles to basic money. They cannot, therefore, create it except in their private capacities as service debtors spending on creditor services.

When a bank makes a loan to a customer and it is drawn, a debt in cash terms has been created. This debt, however, must not be confused with basic money, since the latter is a debt in services. Thus, basic money can only be created by the performance of services.

Now we can try another approach. You are invited to sit in a bank manager's chair and to look at the position from the other side of the desk.

Firstly, you are appointed manager at a small branch, so you have the opportunity to 'create credit, and hence money, by lending'. Unfortunately, the town in question is not thriving. Indeed, the reverse is the case. Some of the industry is closing down and there is an increasing level of unemploymeant. Business is not brisk, but you do manage to make a few loans. To your disappointment, you find that both deposits and advances are falling. Many of your depositors have lost their main sources of income and the flow of funds into their accounts has been reduced. Fewer people are asking for loans and your corporate customers, whose businesses are the mainstay of the town, are contracting their activities. They are drawing decreasing sums weekly for the payment of wages and are making less use of their overdraft facilities for other purposes as well. As regards personal borrowers, your records show that, taken on a monthly basis, repayments being made exceed new loans being granted.

You have, therefore, been unable to 'create credit, and hence money, by lending'. In fact, it could be said that you have done the reverse in terms of that argument. A reduction is taking place in the basic money supply and you are assisting with the process. Fewer notes are required for wage payments and other transactions, so you are able to forward the surplus to the department which handles remittances or, if you receive a weekly supply, to reduce your demand. Either way, the department will have surplus notes and, assuming all other things are equal meantime, will pay them into your bank's account with the Bank of England. The discount houses will borrow the surplus funds but will be unable to lend them. The Bank of England will then mop up the excess by selling Treasury Bills to the discount houses and the reduction in the money supply, basic and nominal, will have been completed.

Now you are in a state! You are losing business and are unable to create money. Not only that, you have been led to believe that a reduction in the money supply is desirable and now you are watching it happen in a way that is obviously not good for the local community. It cannot possibly be of benefit to the country.

Two years later, Head Office takes pity on you and, to your relief, you are moved to a large office where there are several managers. Corporate finance and personal lending are handled separately and you are put in charge of the latter. Business is brisk and by the end of the year you feel you have more than earned your salary. You decide to check back to find out how well you have done and ask a member of your staff to provide figures for the following: (a) lending approved; (b) loans drawn and (c) current borrowing.

As expected, the amounts shown become progressively smaller. Many loans are not taken up. Bridging loans, for example, may not, in the course of events, be required after all and in some cases the sums drawn may be less than those agreed.

Repayments of existing indebtedness keep coming in and, while the average loan may be of, say, two years' duration, this would result, assuming no change in the lending activity and no bad debts, in the current borrowing being half of the loans drawn.

There is no magic formula for the relationship between these figures, but we shall suppose that, in your case, the proportions read as follows:

$$5 : 4 : 2$$

Thus, for every £5 million of lending approved, £4 million is drawn and sustains current borrowing of £2 million. The office of the bank is big enough to provide a cross-section of what is happening in the country. Thus, you discover that instead of every loan creating a deposit, you need to carry out a considerable amount of continuous new lending to prevent deposits and advances from falling. Otherwise, the repayments from creditor accounts will more than offset the new loans.

Once more you are promoted, and this time you are appointed chief manager at a large office where your main responsibility is corporate finance. No sooner have you sat down at your new desk than a boom in trading activity takes place across the country. Deposits and advances rise substantially and at the end of the year you decide to find out how much fresh business you have obtained. To your surprise, the number of new accounts opened is little more than in an average year. You wonder what has caused the increased activity. Then the penny drops. You have simply lent more funds to the corporate borrowers whose accounts were in the office on your arrival.

These customers have increased production, bought more raw materials, employed extra labour and incurred additional overheads. Funds have flowed from debtor to creditor accounts, thereby reflecting the increased basic money supply. Thus, the same participants in the market-place have become more active. The increase in advances and deposits will be entirely healthy as long as more goods and services are being supplied and pay and prices remain stable. There is, therefore, no source from which additional borrowers of consequence can materialise every time there is a boom or a bank has funds to lend.

More cash is needed for the payment of wages, so this time you are assisting in the process by which basic money is created, ie, debtor spending on creditor services.

With experience in managerial chairs behind you, it should be obvious to you that a banker is not a catalyst or a 'creator'. He reacts to the economic climate in his locality and to the trading activity of his customers. He cannot force the pace, though occasionally he can gain business by making his services more attractive, and particularly so if he tailors them to his customers' needs. His own prosperity is tied in with the success of his customers and, consequently, he should always be ready to listen to their propositions and to assist them whenever he can. He does not create basic money and has no need to do so, as the funds he requires for lending are provided by his customers.

Banks are deemed to act as principals rather than as agents. The latter description, however, is more apt when they link the supply of surplus deposits to the demand for borrowing. Thus, by way of comparison, a stockbroker does not create marketable securities, an estate agent does not create houses and a banker, by lending, does not create basic money.

Readers should now be in a position to reject all forms of credit creation theory, no matter how convoluted, both on the basis of their false supporting arguments and in the light of the new knowledge.

Credit

Distinctions are being made at present between Trade Credit and Bank Credit. In the case of the former, it is contended that one party only obtains what the other gives up, whereas, in regard to the latter, credit creation theory is wrongly deemed to apply.

To combat this, let us get the functions of the banks into perspective. They are not needed in small communities. Borrowers know personally the parties from whom they can obtain funds; goods and services are bought from, and sold to, neighbours without the need for market-places. As trade develops, however, these become essential. Dealings are now taking place between parties who do not necessarily know one another. Larger sums are being accumulated and safe places are needed in which to keep them. This requirement was first met by the strongboxes of the goldsmiths and later by the vaults of the banks. Thus, the need for the banks' services comes before they commence operations. The demand is not for a source of new funds, but for a market-place where existing funds can be deposited and borrowed. The banks take over the lending function, but did not invent it.

If banks were able to create credit, and hence money, by lending, every town or village with a bank branch would automatically grow. In fact, if local industry, which was the reason for a town's existence, fails, many shops and sometimes the local bank branch close down. The demand for their services has fallen and they are no longer economic propositions. That is why ghost towns result.

The banks are an essential feature of our present state of development, but their sizes are determined by their ability to provide services in response to demand and to sell new ones. The ability to create basic money by granting credit is not among them. In effect, depositors lend their basic money supply credits to the banks; the latter do not have to make immediate repayment and are, therefore, being given credit by the former. The amount of credit being given is equal to that being obtained and, in consequence, there is no net creation of credit. The same principle applies when banks lend their depositors' credits to their borrowers. No party can add to the amount of credit being given without simultaneously adding, to the same extent, to the amount of credit being obtained. One offsets the other.

Many people seem to believe that credit is a modern form of money. In truth, of course, it is not money of any description and by the nature of things is endemic in the production of goods and the provision of services. It was present in barter societies, just as much as it is today.

Donald, a farmer, rears cattle and considers that one of his calves is surplus to requirements. He decides to take it to the next market in the hope of exchanging it for something he would rather possess.

Unbeknown to him, Edward, another farmer, who rears pigs, has a similar problem. He has too many piglets and has made up his mind to take three of them to the market. In the event, the pair meet and to their mutual satisfaction the calf is exchanged for the little pigs.

When one person performs a service for the benefit of another, however unwittingly, without payment, he is giving credit and the second one is receiving it to the same extent. Thus, Donald and Edward were both giving and receiving credit prior to the exchange. They were performing the services of rearing and tending animals for each other's benefit.

If Edward had gone to the market without taking his surplus livestock and been given the calf on the understanding that he would deliver the piglets in seven days' time, he would clearly be receiving extended credit from Donald over that period. This credit then appears to exceed the other, but it should be borne in mind that Edward is giving credit by continuing to rear and tend Donald's piglets during the extra week. As always, therefore, there is no net creation of credit.

When a person performs a service, which will be paid for in due course, credit is created. Thus, a clerk gives his employer credit until pay day by performing his duties during the intervening period. When someone performs useful services for a charitable organisation without payment, credit is being created and gifted to it. If, however, services are valueless, there is no creation of credit.

An individual may earn more from his services than he spends, so the question arises as to whether or not this is a net creation of credit. Again, the answer is in the negative. Other parties have gained to the extent that he has not taken out all he could from society.

Manufacturers give credit to the eventual consumers by producing goods without demanding advance or stage payments. In the case of a hire purchase transaction, the existing credit is extended. The hire purchase company is probably operating with borrowed funds and pays the supplier. Nevertheless, ultimate settlement of the outstanding debt, for which basic money is necessary, has not been effected.

Credit and basic money are, therefore, two different things. The former allows us to run up debts and to live beyond our immediate means; the latter enables us to make purchases and to settle debts.

It has been contended that credit has to a large extent replaced money as a medium of exchange; further, since it acts as such a medium, it is said to be money.

When a hire purchase transaction is carried out, an exchange undoubtedly takes place, but it is on the understanding that payment will be made later and ownership is only transferred with the last instalment. Basic money, not a medium of exchange, is the means of settlement, even though it comes in the form of future income. The fact that goods can be obtained on credit highlights the need for precise definitions of basic and nominal money.

In the foregoing example, the ownership of the goods remained with the hire purchase company until the final instalment was paid. Another question is, therefore, prompted. If ownership is transferred at once, is there a difference?

Frederick, who wishes to purchase a house, approaches a building society, obtains a loan, grants a mortgage and undertakes to effect repayment over a period of 20 years. The property is registered in his name and he is the legal owner. Has the loan acted as a medium of exchange? Again, the answer is in the negative. In terms of the agreement, basic money supply credits, probably represented by a bank draft, were provided for the purpose of settlement.

The amount of credit has been growing over the years. So much so that it has become a national issue, a matter of adverse comment by the media and a source of concern to the monetary authorities. Whenever credit is mentioned, however, all the attention focuses on the parties who obtain it, the borrowers, and little or no notice is taken of the suppliers. Thus, the perspective has been completely lost.

Who are the suppliers? The retailers? – no. The finance companies? – no. The building societies? – no. The commercial banks? – no. Who then? Depositors. Yes, deposits are the source of all credit given and these too have been growing annually. Depositors place their funds with banks, building societies and the other deposit-takers and by that action give credit to those organisations.

Retailers often give credit to their customers. Some are service creditors and can do so from their own resources – their deposits. Most, however, are borrowers and use depositors' funds for the purpose, which they obtain from banks.

The finance companies take deposits directly from the public, when licensed to do so, and often obtain deposits from the banks in the form of overdrafts, short term fixtures and term loans. Moreover, they often have arrangements whereby they draw bills of exchange on banks, which are accepted by those organisations and discounted by the discount houses; the funds the houses use for this purpose have been obtained from the banks. Again, we find that the suppliers are, however indirectly, the banks' depositors.

Building societies finance the purchase of houses and extensions to them, while banks lend for a multiplicity of reasons. Both types of organisation use their depositors' funds for these purposes.

Loans have to be kept in existence until borrowers are ready to repay them, so the settlement system must cover this situation. Suppose that George wishes to buy a house. He borrows the purchase price from his friend, Harry, and undertakes to repay the loan in ten equal yearly instalments. It would be clear that, for every day of the borrowing, Harry would be giving up the outstanding purchasing power obtained by George.

The situation is the same if the loan is granted by a bank or a building society, but it is the purchasing power not being used immediately by many and changing depositors which provides the necessary cover on a daily basis. One might say that borrowers have many more friends than they are aware of!

A time element is, of course, involved and can range from one day to a considerable number of years. There is, however, no difference in principle in financing, say, a 25-year mortgage loan or weekly housekeeping, perhaps over a similar period! Remember that lenders borrow their working capital from their depositors and have no funds of their own available for this purpose.

Every penny of credit given is thus supported by deposits. It is true that these deposits are turning over, but those lost are replaced by others and the cover remains intact.

Economic conditions cause people to react in different ways. Many take the view that in inflationary conditions they should borrow as much as they can, particularly in respect of houses. The rich, however, often become more concerned about finding ways of preserving their wealth; the comparatively rich and those seeking this status can become careful and thrifty and those on fixed incomes are obliged to spend less. Moreover, many people will do almost anything to avoid reducing their nest eggs, no matter how poor they are or what hardship they have to endure to this end. It must be remembered that basic money supply credits run to the hands of the rich and high income earners; lots of these people live very comfortably and well within their incomes. The end result of these behavioural patterns is that there is a constant inflow of new deposits and outflow of old ones.

Organisations use the double-entry book-keeping system. If credit could be given unilaterally, the books involved would not balance. Credit in itself is not, therefore, a cause of inflation.

Service creditors, as well as service debtors, use credit cards. As a result, total advances in the books of the credit card companies include balances which will be cleared before the due dates, and, in respect of the relevant sums, deposits elsewhere contain an element of overstatement. The credit card companies have access to similar facilities from the banks as the other finance ones and the source of their funds, deposits, is the same.

The supply of credit is limited by the availability of deposits. If the demand for borrowing becomes too high, interest rates are put up. The weaker would-be borrowers are then priced out of the market. In other words, supply and demand are kept in balance by the interest rates. That is their proper function.

Reckless lending results in losses to the lenders and the destruction of BMSC and BMSD to the same extent. Thus, in a bankruptcy or liquidation, creditors lose whatever debtors are unable to pay. Losses on a large scale can, therefore, be a serious matter for the community.

The conclusions are inevitable. Credit is endemic in all transactions. The amount given equals that received, whether Trade Credit or Bank Credit. One party gives up what another obtains. Credit cannot act as a means of settlement or as a medium of exchange. Its importance lies in the facts that it allows some parties to live beyond their immediate means, it permits a higher level of trading activity to be achieved and it results in a raised standard of living. Provided parties do not overcommit themselves, it is, like prudent bank lending, entirely healthy.

The functions of money

Money has been defined as anything which acts as a medium of exchange, a unit of account or a store of value; moreover, the corollary is that items which perform such functions are money. In the light, however, of our new knowledge, neither the definition nor the corollary is tenable.

A medium of exchange is needed to evidence the existence of intangible basic money and to transfer it. In addition, a means of measuring it, a unit of account, is required. Thus, in practice, basic money is jointly a credit and a debt in services, cash and cheques are media of exchange and the pound and the dollar are units of account. Basic money, media of exchange and units of account are, therefore, three different things.

Basic money does not perform the function of a unit of account, which is simply a measure. In the example regarding the farmer and the horse-seller, basic money was the credit and debt in services, the medium of exchange was a marker and the unit of account was a sack of wheat. When trade is carried on with the aid of a commodity in common use, such as tobacco, the item in question serves as a medium of exchange and a given quantity of it as a unit of account.

It is basic money which acts as a store of value, and not the medium of exchange nor the unit of account. The criterion is the ownership of the service credits. Unfortunately, the value of basic money can be eroded by inflation.

We are told that bags of salt, cigarettes, gold and many other items were used in past times to perform the functions attributed to money. In fact, these things served as media of exchange and quantities of them as units of account. Trade has always been carried out in services and the commodities were used to evidence the existence of basic money and to transfer it. The true position has not been appreciated.

The stock of gold and the basic money supply were not the same thing. When borrowed gold was spent by a service debtor on creditor services, an addition was made to the basic money supply, while the stock of gold was unchanged. Equally, when gold was spent by a service creditor on debtor services, basic money supply was destroyed, but again the stock was unaltered.

People trade only in services. We are, however, in the habit of distinguishing between the work they do in manufacturing goods and in performing unproductive services. It should be borne in mind, therefore, that references in the text to goods and services still means services only and are made simply in recognition of common practice.

Basically, people still want to exchange goods and services for the things they want, that is, to barter. Thus, when they accept monetary reward for goods and/or services, only part of the process of barter has taken place; when they, in turn, buy goods and/or services, the process is complete. With the use of basic money, they can buy goods and/or services in quantities approximating to their needs and at the times required. The whole process is possible because basic money bridges the gap in time. Basic money, media of exchange and units of account are refinements added to the bartering system, and so is banking.

Money could not have been better designed if its function were to deceive! The time for its unmasking has long been overdue.

The Quantity Theory of Money

Briefly stated, this theory holds that prices vary in sympathy with the quantity of money. Thus, if that quantity is increased or reduced, prices will rise and fall respectively by like percentages.

The theory falls to be examined (a) in terms of its contentions and supporting arguments and (b) in the light of our new knowledge. For purposes of comparison, the points have been numbered, sections headed (a) referring to present teaching and belief (unilateral monetary theory) and those under (b) to the new concepts (bilateral monetary theory).

1(a). Money is assumed to be a stock, the main constituents of which are cash and bank deposits.

(b) Basic money is the net result of the processes of continuous creation and destruction and is better described as a flow. The outstanding balance is made up equally on the one side of service credits and on the other of service debts. Cash is nominal money and bank deposits are book-keeping records.

2(a). A bank with the right to issue notes can increase its circulation unilaterally and permanently by printing more notes and using them to purchase goods and services; the result is an increase to the same extent in cash and bank deposits.

(b) Banks are service debtors and only their spending on creditor services increases the basic money supply. Suppose that a note-issuing bank decides to print extra notes to the value of £10 million, that it uses this sum to have its branches modernised, that the firms employed on the work have their accounts with the bank, that 30 per cent of the funds are paid into creditor accounts, that the rest are paid into debtor ones and that the bank is operating on a fixed liquidity ratio.

The basic money supply has been increased by £3 million and is reflected by the rise in deposits. The liquidity ratio is now too low, so the bank sells £3 million of investments to depositors.

The bank has not, therefore, succeeded in its purpose. It has been forced to replace earning assets – advances of £7 million and investments worth £3 million – by non-earning assets in the form of fixtures and fittings. It has not been able to create money and has lost part of its income. Its experience is exactly the same as that of an individual who spends part of his capital on refurnishing his house.

It is the right of the public to determine the quantity of the note circulation and not the issuing bank. In a free society, it is not possible to foist onto parties more cash than they demand and unwanted notes will be returned for redemption.

Extra cash is demanded by the public for two main reasons, the first to finance an increase in trading activity and the second to obtain more pay for doing the same, or proportionally less, work. The first situation is healthy, but the second is undesirable. In both cases, the authority does not issue notes unilaterally; it does so in response to demand. The notes can, therefore, go into circulation. Owing to the status rules, however, the result can never be 'an increase to the same extent in cash and bank deposits'.

3(a). The Quantity Theory of Money is often expressed as MV =

PT, where M is money, V is velocity of circulation, P is the average price of transactions and T is the number of transactions.

(b) M in the equation is not basic money, which is subject to continuous creation and destruction, cannot be measured, is specific to the parties creating it, does not circulate and can only be used once. The equation, therefore, does not deal with the facts.

Raw materials and produce are provided by nature without charge. Only parties demand payment and costs are comprised solely of their impositions. Average price multiplied by number of transactions simply equals total costs and not money supply.

An equation representing the basic money supply could read: X − Y = Z, where X is money created, Y is money destroyed and Z is the outstanding balance. It would be clear that the resulting Z figures would be a reflection of the trading activity and not a catalyst capable of influencing the economy.

Z would be comprised of outstanding basic money supply credits and would equal the cost of transactions resulting from debtor spending on creditor services, the debt element of which has not yet been redeemed. This situation may be of interest, but, like the Quantity Theory, has no economic consequences.

4(a). The value of money is determined by its quantity. Thus, increases reduce the purchasing power of the unit of account and reductions have the opposite effect.

(b) The value of basic money is determined by the behaviour of the participants in the trading activity. The services, which created basic money, have been performed and are unalterable. They were, however, valued in a unit of account. Consequently, if the unit of account is debased or refined, a new value is put upon the services. For example, *ceteris paribus*, pay increases for doing the same, or comparatively less, work debase the unit of account, while pay cuts for doing the same, or proportionally more, work refine it.

The value of basic money can, therefore, be altered by actions which take place outside the monetary and banking systems. Those which lower the value of the unit of account result in a loss of purchasing power by service creditors and a corresponding reduction in the obligations of service debtors; those which raise the value of the unit of account have the opposite effects.

When the new money being created has, on average, lesser or greater purchasing power than the rest of the basic money supply, the value of the latter has automatically to come into line. Consider this point carefully, as it is of major importance. The same printing presses can be used to depreciate the currency or to strengthen it. The laws governing the quantity of basic money are not those of supply and demand.

The value of the new money being created is determined by the pay and price structure. Thus, that structure is the key to the economy and the only lever by which it can be managed efficiently. Successful economic measures have to affect human behaviour and not its reflections.

The Quantity Theory of Money can no longer be taken seriously and readers should now be able to reject any contentions based upon it, including monetarism.

The Theory of the Velocity of Circulation of Money

It has been contended that changes in the velocity of circulation of money affect its value. Thus, it is said that if velocity is increased, price levels will rise in the same way as they have been deemed to do when the quantity of money appears to have been increased unilaterally. This is based on the notion that if money works harder, the result will be more money chasing the same quantity of goods and services.

The advocates of the theory believe that money supply is made up mainly of cash and bank deposits. Moreover, they are unaware of the differences between basic money and media of exchange. With an incorrect assessment of the nature of money as their starting point, it is inevitable that they have ended up with a number of false conclusions.

We already know that the quantity of money is not the catalyst in the raising of prices. A question has, however, been prompted. Can money work harder?

Reconsider the true position. Every transaction alters the constituent parts of the basic money supply and those between parties of different statuses change its amount. Basic money is created by debtor spending on creditor services and destroyed by creditor spending on debtor services. A service creditor spending on creditor services reduces basic money supply credits, while the other party to the transaction increases them simultaneously by an equal amount; a service debtor spending on debtor services increases basic money supply debts, while the other party to the transaction reduces them by an equal amount. These facts show that money can only be used once and cannot, therefore, work harder.

Generally speaking, parties are fairly regular in their spending habits. There are times, however, when they are, on balance, either optimistic or pessimistic about the direction the economy is taking. In the first circumstance, they spend more and, in the second, less. Booms and recessions result. Supporters of the theory maintain that the velocity of circulation of money rises and falls in booms and recessions respectively. This, however, is incorrect. Booms result in basic money supply credits being spent faster than they can be created by the performance of services. Consequently, booms cannot be sustained. In recessions, debtor spending is cut back and less basic money is being created. Changes in the rate of spending have wrongly been interpreted as money working harder or less hard.

Spending is sometimes diverted to new products at the expense of old ones and fashion may favour sections of an industry to the detriment of the rest. On some occasions, trade cycles affect industry generally, but on others, various industries can be at different stages of such cycles. We are dealing with a living situation and movement constantly takes place. People, in spite of the basic nature of their needs, are not entirely predictable. Demand and production can, as a result, get out of step and have to be reconciled to one another. The adjustments should not be taken to be increases and reductions in the velocity of circulation of money.

Media of exchange can be reused, but, strictly speaking, not circulated. The oil lubricating parts of an engine and the hot water in a central heating system circulate, the essence of the situation being that they are not impeded. Media of exchange, on the other hand, are more like arrows fired from a bow. Each one serves a specific purpose and some can be reused. They travel from point to point, but spend most of their time dormant in quivers. Thus, they cannot circulate and the question of velocity in such a context does not arise.

Remember that media of exchange can change their allegiance. In the hands of a service creditor, they represent purchasing power, but become evidence of the destruction of basic money supply debts on being acquired by service debtors. In terms of the analogy, an arrow can be shot back!

In periods of great inflation, monetary authorities have spewed out a seemingly endless supply of cash in response to public demand and banking systems have had to cope with rapidly increasing figures in ledgers. Workers have even received their wages on an hourly basis. This, however, is not an increase in velocity of circulation, as only an hour's work is being remunerated each time.

Here is an accounting example which purports to prove the theory.

Albert is paid £1,200 in cash every four weeks and deposits the funds in his bank account. He spends £300 per week and his average balance over every four-week period is £600. His employer, Ben, decides to pay him £600 per fortnight and his average balance drops to £300. This sum is then deemed to be doing the work of £600 and the velocity of circulation is assumed to have increased.

Again, it has not been appreciated that basic money is bilateral and that there has to be an effect also on Ben's balance.

Assume that he, too, has an average creditor balance of £600, when Albert is paid every four weeks. After the change, *ceteris paribus*, this average would become £900. Increased velocity in the first case would be cancelled by its reduction in the second.

Now suppose instead that Ben has an average overdraft of £600. On the changeover, it would fall to £300. All that has been proved is that if parties settled their debts more often, the economy could be financed with a smaller basic money supply. Since deposits and advances would both be down, the liquidity ratio would be marginally higher and the £300 reduction in Ben's overdraft could be lent elsewhere. The net result of the inconvenience in increasing the frequency of wage payments should also be noted.

Velocity of circulation is not involved in the processes by which basic money is created and destroyed and can never be more, or less, than one.

The equation MV = PT contains two misconceptions, the first that basic money supply is a stock and, the second, that it can have a velocity of circulation other than one.

The Theory of the Velocity of Circulation of Money can now join The Quantity Theory of Money on the list of unsound concepts.

The 'Multiplier'

It has been contended that additional government expenditure can cause a 'multiplier' effect to ripple through the economy. Thus, if new buildings are commissioned, the contractors will purchase raw materials, pay wages, incur expenses, employ other firms, increase dividends etc. The funds disbursed are deemed to work their way through the economy and cause extra production on being spent by the recipients. The increase in output will then be more than just the buildings and in value may be, say, three times as great. The multiplier would than be three. Unfortunately, the funds for the original expenditure were plucked out of the air and, if one starts with a false premise, the result is an incorrect conclusion.

The government is a service debtor and to get more funds has to increase taxes or borrowing. The taxpayers or the lenders have to divert the funds from their existing uses, so one ripple dries up to allow the new one to take its place. In these circumstances, benefits from government expenditure are mythical. Moreover, the same argument applies to government investment.

In any case, the events are inadequately described. The main suppliers of goods and services are service debtors, so the transactions would only result in, say, a 30 per cent increase in basic money, a much lower effect than envisaged.

The lesson is clear. The government should only finance projects which are likely to be of benefit; it should not engage in the business of Santa Claus.

Labour costs

It is often said that labour costs are a part, say 20 per cent, of total costs. Raw materials and produce are provided free by nature and only parties charge for their services. Thus, all payments go to them in one capacity or another, either as pay or prices. Labour costs are, therefore, 100 per cent of total costs.

Enslavement

The monetary system has been accused of many things and one of the more unusual is that people are enslaved by it. In fact, it is their need to forage for their basic requirements – food, clothing, heating and shelter – which does this. The monetary system allows most of us to obtain these requirements, to enjoy some luxuries and to attain, through trading activity, a standard of living which would otherwise be well out of reach. In truth, the important issue is to ensure that no one is excluded from adequate access to the monetary system.

Interest rates

The function of interest rates is to hold the ring between the demand for borrowing and the supply of deposits available for lending. If the demand increases, interest rates should be raised to price the weaker would-be borrowers out of the market; if it falls, interest rates should be reduced to encourage borrowing. It is vital that the deposits available for lending should be fully utilised, for otherwise the trading activity will fall and with it the standard of living.

These are very important principles and interference with such normal and healthy practices in the market-place can only be damaging. Indeed, it is completely irresponsible to use the interest rates for any other purpose.

It is wrong, therefore, to increase them to defend sterling exchange rates. That worsens the position by making the economy less competitive. Countries trading at a loss should cut pay and prices. Speculators would not then gamble against the currency.

Equally unsound are the beliefs, widely held by monetary authorities, that alterations to interest rates can usefully be made to affect demand and inflation and, moreover, that they are necessary for the pursuit of price stability.

Such authorities, acting on these misconceptions, are attempting to deal with a situation which does not exist. There is no monetary phenomenon; demand need not be damped down; and pay and prices policy could both eliminate inflation and provide price stability.

Demand is financed by borrowing, and increases in it do not have to be accompanied by inflation. It should, therefore, be accommodated unless this can only be done at the expense of more desirable lending.

Sovereign lending

Many bankers have questioned the wisdom of making loans to other countries. Normal lending principles require that the banker should have sound reasons for believing that repayment will be made as agreed and that security can be taken beforehand as a safeguard against events not following their predicted course. Yet neither of these conditions is available in the case of sovereign lending. The lender is, in fact, entirely dependent on the borrower.

It is recognised that many of the loans coming under this description are made under pressure for reasons of politics, diplomacy or friendship. That, however, is all the more reason for resisting unsound propositions. A true friend tells you when you are in the wrong and refuses to go along with schemes which are likely to turn out to your disadvantage.

In practice, a competent lending banker rarely has to say, 'No'. He either agrees to his customer's proposals because they are sound, or explains what is wrong with them. Sometimes the proposals can be suitably amended, but, if not, the customer usually sees the light and withdraws them.

The developing countries have to learn to trade more, both at home and abroad, if they want to progress, and this is the issue which must be discussed with them rather than the granting of loans. Since the power to create basic money lies with the individual, whether acting alone or in concert with others, every nation can generate its own wealth. Borrowing basic money for unsound reasons is not the road to prosperity: it is a short cut to ruin.

Lessons on bank lending

There are three important lessons to be learned in regard to bank lending, which are as follows:

(1) It is unsound policy for the monetary authorities to attempt to restrict bank lending.

Restrictions were imposed in the mistaken belief that banks create money by lending and that such activities cause inflation.

They led to a market developing in inter-company loans. Thus, one company would lend its surplus funds to another, which was the same part of its creditor balance its bank would have used for a similar purpose had the preventative measures not been in force. In this fashion, other lenders were encouraged to engage in the business of the banks.

The restrictions were futile, as they did not necessarily constrain lending and were harmful to the extent that they did. Moreover, their imposition gave the false impression that there is something damaging in the normal lending activities of the banks. In fairness, the record should be set to rights.

For the attainment of economic growth, it is necessary that our spare funds should be collected and lent to finance the production of goods and the supply of services. In addition, the need for more direct investment in industry is recognised; it is not enough for one party to buy stocks and shares from another, as that practice, remember, is simply dealing in company debt.

In general, direct investment provides permanent capital and bank lending supplies working capital. Restrictions can deprive business and industry of working capital at times when more investment is advocated. There is no logic in this. Without adequate working capital, companies experience difficulty in making profits. Who is interested in making direct investments in unprofitable ones?

Another error was the restriction of dividend payments. These are made from profits already earned and there is nothing inflationary in this practice. They are the reward for lending funds to companies and they are no different from interest from government securities, except for the way in which they are calculated. Direct investment, including foreign, is discouraged by the restrictions as issues of stocks and shares cannot be made attractive enough. In a competitive world we cannot afford to hamper business and industry in this way.

The banks already have restrictions of their own on lending. They are careful in vetting borrowers, do not make advances unless they have good reason to expect repayment in full plus interest and frequently ask beforehand for security as a form of insurance against events not following their predicted course. Bank managers are sitting in judgement on a major part of the economic activities of the community and, to some extent, influence what goods and services parties can buy.

If the banks overlend, surplus production could result. Some customers would then be unable to sell enough of their goods, would incur losses and would fail to meet their obligations to the banks. On the other hand, too little lending could result in shortages of goods. How can arbitrary restrictions, imposed by guesswork and based on false premises, improve the situation? Clearly, it is folly to restrict practices which facilitate trade.

(2) Economic policy must be aimed at lowering the cost of production (cost of services) and increasing its level.

A percentage cut in pay and prices would have this effect. Fewer notes would be required for the payment of wages and the surplus ones would be returned to the Bank of England's Issue Department. The outstanding basic money supply credits would gain in value and the holders would be tempted to increase their spending. Production could be increased and more goods sold at lower prices.

No monetary or fiscal policy can achieve this essential combination.

(3) The target for monetary and economic policy must be future earnings and not bank deposits, bank lending or false money supply.

As we shall discover, the problem of eliminating inflation narrows down to how to prevent people being paid ever-increasing sums for doing the same, or a comparatively less, amount of work.

6

Inflation

The prominent place of inflation

The subject of inflation could justifiably have been included in the previous chapter, as there are many misconceptions in respect of it. It has, however, occupied such a prominent place in unilateral monetary theory that it has been deemed to warrant a separate chapter.

Again, in discussing false theories, 'money' is used in accordance with normal practice.

The sole cause of inflation

People trade solely in services. Consequently, only increases in the average charges for those services cause inflation. Thus, its sole cause is our 'success' in pursuing our insatiable desire to be paid ever-increasing sums of debased basic money for doing the same, or a relatively lesser, amount of work.

As a general rule, inflation is not caused by the actions of the government, the practices of the monetary authorities or the operations of the banks. There is, however, one exception. Each of these groups contributes to inflation in its capacity as an employer of labour.

It is sometimes said that inflation is caused by a number of factors. This is simply not true. We do not trade in factors other than services. Consequently, the values placed on those services determine whether the country experiences inflation, deflation or stable conditions.

The precise definitions of inflation and deflation

Revert to the transactions between A and B. Suppose that before the reciprocal service is performed, B is able to insist on it being reduced; the credit becomes less valuable and the debt less burdensome; inflation has resulted.

Alternatively, assume that A can insist on a greater service being carried out; the credit gains in value and the debt becomes more burdensome; deflation has ensued.

Thus inflation and deflation occur in economies before and after monetary systems are in operation; indeed, the introduction of one merely allows their extents to be measured in cash terms. Inflation cannot, therefore, be a monetary phenomenon.

Suppose that the agreement between A and B was that each should perform ten hours' work. During the intervening period, cash is introduced to their community and their labour is valued at £1 per hour. The debt is fixed at £10. Owing, however, to pay and prices being pushed up, their work becomes valued at £1.25 per hour by the time B is due to reciprocate. He gets away with repaying the debt with eight hours' work. A has been cheated. Either he accepts eight hours' work in settlement or he pays £2.50 for the other two hours.

If, instead, pay and prices had been pushed down, so that an hour's work was valued at 80p, B would be the one to have been cheated. He would have had to work for $12\frac{1}{2}$ hours to clear the £10 debt due to A.

The rates of inflation and deflation can now be calculated in terms of the unit of account, but could already be worked out in terms of hours. Thus, the forces causing inflation and deflation are outside the monetary system.

It is alterations in trading conditions which cause inflation or deflation, while the respective falls and rises in the value of the unit of account are simply reflections. Accordingly, the precise definition of inflation is a varying bias in the terms of trade favouring the service debtors, and that of deflation is a varying bias in the terms of trade favouring the service creditors.

Inflation in modern economies

How then does inflation arise in modern economies? It is caused by employers granting pay increases and recouping the cost from increased prices. Remember that all payments are made to parties and that labour is 100 per cent of costs. Only pay and prices fall to be considered, as they are the rewards for the performance of services. The wider description, 'income and expenditure', includes transfers such as dividends, gifts, legacies and taxes.

Increases in the pay level added to prices (inflation) reduce the value of the service credits and the burden of the service debts, while reductions in the pay level taken from prices (deflation) increase the value of the service credits and the burden of the service debts. Thus, the purchasing power per pound of the outstanding service credits can vary over periods of time and has to come into line continuously with the average value of the new service credits being created or, in other words, with current prices. That principle applies whether the new credits have more or less value per pound than the old ones.

Service credits and service debts retain their nominal values. In consequence, a service debt of, say, £100 can be wiped out by the payment of this sum, even though the pound has gained or lost in value prior to settlement. Total service credits still equal total service debts, but the total current purchasing power of the service credits will not equal the total original burdens of the service debts, except in the most freakish of circumstances. Thus, in inflationary conditions, service debtors can wipe out their obligations by performing services of lesser value than originally obtained. That is why so many people were able to buy houses with mortgage loans and ended up owning properties the current values of which are several times the purchase prices.

All the features which show up when a monetary system is introduced are already present in the economy. The undesirable ones should not, therefore, be laid at the doors of the monetary system, the banking procedures or the printing presses. Paper currencies are a great boon. We must, however, learn how to manage and protect them.

Buyers and sellers

All trade, whether in goods or services, involves buyers and sellers. The aim of economic policy must, therefore, be to bring the market forces between them into a desirable form of monetary equilibrium and to maintain that state of affairs. If the sellers gain the upper hand, inflation results, while, if the buyers prevail, deflation ensues.

One can easily be misled into believing that the economy is all about employers and employees rather than buyers and sellers, because of the extensive media coverage given to industrial relations. It should be noted, therefore, that employers and employees are on the same side – the sellers' one – and that their squabbles are internal family affairs when compared with the wider issues. Indeed, payments of remuneration are agreements between employers and employees in their capacities as sellers in the market-place, whereas sales of goods and services are transactions between buyers and sellers.

Successive governments have allowed the sellers to weight the scales on their own side, although this has not been in the real interests of the workforces or the country.

Every year scientific and technological advances make it easier and cheaper to provide for the existing standard of living. This should mean that the basic money supply would gain in purchasing power, that the rate of inflation would be negative and that the benefits would be shared by the entire population. As it is, the workforces are acquiring these benefits for themselves, so measures to achieve an equilibrium are desirable.

Charts are sometimes produced showing the rates of inflation over various periods of time. These are often used to support contentions such as monetarism, the grounds being that policies have influenced the rates. This is not the case. The rates merely show to some extent the advantage the sellers have had in the market-place. They understate the position, because of the acquisition by the sellers of the benefits of scientific and technological advances.

Inflation would be of little importance if all parties were active in the market-place, both in selling services and buying requirements. There would be a natural equilibrium. This is not, however, the way things are.

All sellers are also buyers, but the converse is not true. Buyers include parties who rely on transferred income and/or savings, such as the unemployed, the retired, the incapacitated, charities and children. These parties can be classified for ease of reference as 'economic dependants'. Inflation cheats them, reduces the value of savings and may force the sale of assets; it continually destroys part of the basic money supply, causes some unemployment and ensures that the economy always underperforms.

Business and industry, not government, control our free market economy. Owing to the avarice of management, aspirations of workers and expectations of shareholders, they have an in-built tendency to be uncompetitive. They could have avoided the last recession by cutting pay and prices, but did not choose to take that course of action. The inevitable setback destroyed part of our economy and left a tranche of companies in the position that their markets had contracted. In an attempt to survive and to retain market share, they dispensed with some employees, reorganised their structures, improved their working practices and offered unsustainable discounts. The pendulum swung temporarily, but not entirely, in favour of the buyers.

The latest techniques of business and industry, known as 'downsizing', are to sell fringe subsidiaries and to concentrate on core activities. Their negative nature should be noted.

In our economy the sellers have had the upper hand for a very long time. The need, therefore, is to take action against them in order to tip the scales in favour of the buyers.

An example worth looking at again is the housing market. Credit is a comparatively scarce resource. Banks and building societies should, therefore, have seen the need to limit mortgage loans to, say, $2\frac{1}{2}$ times one salary and, when more than one was available for repayments, to shorten the periods of the loans. More house purchases could then have been financed at lower prices. As it was, every advantage apparently being given to the buyers by way of increased loans and mortgage interest relief merely allowed them to pay more and created a monstrous sellers' market. Both the lenders and the government intended to help the buyers, but that is not what happened. Excessive prices were paid for property and land, interest rates were raised and both these occurrences were to the detriment of industrial and other borrowers, actual or intending. Worse still, the penalty is being paid in part by many of the present generation of borrowing house-buyers, who find that the current values of their homes are less than their mortgage loans, the situation described as 'negative equity'. In addition, all these experiences have led to the unsound notion that the housing market is only healthy when prices are rising.

What are the monetary authorities for, if not to step in when such a market was going so obviously astray? They were, as good monetarists, relying on the interest rates. Well, now experience shows that this is a classic example of the misuse of valuable credit and the ineptitude of monetary policy.

There was some excuse for the banks and building societies, as they are competing for business, but none for the authorities. The economy needs to be managed if it is to achieve its full capacity, and not be left to chance. Indeed, it has to be organised on the basis that, as part of the workforces, we provide for the economic dependants as well as ourselves and, in return, we will be cared for, when we no longer perform services. The market forces have, therefore, to be weighted in favour of the buyers to the extent necessary to achieve this desirable end. It transpires that more than an equilibrium is required or, in other words, one allowing for the buyers' disadvantages.

In inflationary conditions, the equilibrium must be weighted in favour of the buyers; in moderate deflationary conditions, the position must be held there; and in greater deflationary conditions, the equilibrium must be weighted in favour of the sellers. For convenience, we can describe the requirement as the 'weighted equilibrium'.

Major inflations

Advocates of the Quantity Theory of Money maintain that large and continuing increases in the quantity of money will boost demand, increase spending and cause inflation.

These results certainly appeared to ensue in Spain in the 16th century, when comparatively large quantities of gold and silver were imported from the New World. The contention has, therefore, seemed to be correct. That, however, was before we understood the differences between basic and nominal money. How does the contention fare now?

Gold and silver can be used as media of exchange since they are often readily acceptable for the settlement of transactions. Alternatively, they can be exchanged for such titles to basic money. Nevertheless, they are not basic money itself, which can only be created by debtor spending on creditor services. Remember that the act of spending is the criterion in the creation and destruction of basic money. Consequently, the importing of gold and silver did not increase the quantity of basic money.

What it did was to increase demand, for the returning adventurers were now very wealthy in terms of material, as opposed to financial, assets. Production, however, was not adequate to meet both existing and new demand. The market forces were tipped strongly in favour of sellers.

In these circumstances, sellers have some options. For example, they could (1) cause inflation by raising prices, (2) increase production while leaving prices unchanged, or (3) leave production and prices at existing levels. The Spaniards chose to raise prices. In so doing, they priced some of the would-be buyers out of the market and accommodated the new demand instead. Thus, the price increases were the cause of inflation and not the imaginary enlarged quantity of basic money.

If the Spaniards had maintained prices and stepped up production, there would have been some delay before supply and demand were again in balance. Nevertheless, the end results would have been well worthwhile. The level of trading activity would have risen and greater prosperity would have ensued. Basic money would have been increased in step and more jobs would have been created. Yes, such increases are, contrary to popular belief, entirely beneficial.

The third option – leaving production and prices unchanged – would have resulted in a form of rationing. There would never have been enough goods and services to meet the demand. Any benefits gained by the adventurers would have been at the expense of the rest of the community.

Now we can see that the experiences of the Spaniards do not support the contention that large and continuing increases in the quantity of money will boost demand, increase spending and cause inflation, since no such increase took place. Indeed, it is clear that it is prices, not the quantity of basic money, which can get out of line. Consequently, in managing an economy, the need is to push them in whatever direction is desirable, though continual control would be an excessive action. Prices are, of course, made up of the cost of services or, in other words, remuneration, so we cannot escape the inevitable conclusion that we need an earnings policy rather than an incomes one.

Inflation, as I have demonstrated, can take place whether or not a monetary system is in operation. It cannot, therefore, be a monetary phenomenon. The contention that it is, however, has had such worldwide publicity that further comments on its supporting arguments are deemed desirable. Indeed, I have been challenged in the course of my writings to find any inflation of major magnitude that has *not* been accompanied or preceded by a major increase in the quantity of money.

To study the effect of a particular issue, it is necessary to ensure that all other things are equal. Suppose that the members of a community are carrying out exactly similar transactions on a weekly basis and that the sellers are increasing prices by a small regular percentage.

Sellers would continually borrow more funds to finance each

tranche of production, would draw extra cash for the payment of wages and would raise prices to recoup the additional costs.

Economic dependent buyers would lose purchasing power, fewer goods would be sold and some unemployment would result. Production would be cut and become relatively more expensive, because of the loss of some of the economies of size. The sellers made redundant would become economic dependent buyers.

The outstanding basic money supply would grow in amount as the process of creation and destruction continued, but its purchasing power in real terms would be falling. Remember that the value of the unit of account has to come into line continuously with the purchasing power of the new basic money being created.

Nominal money, too, would increase in amount, but would be required for fewer transactions. It is tied in with basic money and has no separate existence. Consequently, in spite of appearances, total nominal money would be losing value in real terms.

Put another way, inflated basic and nominal money at the end of a period would have less value than the basic and nominal money in use at its beginning.

Clearly, the catalyst is the increase in prices and not the growing quantity of basic money. Such money cannot create itself and is the result of the trading conditions.

No inflation of major magnitude has, therefore, been accompanied or preceded by a major increase in the quantity of basic or nominal money in real terms. Price increases are responsible for every step along the way.

The correct way to cure inflation is for the government to cut all remuneration and insist on the savings in costs being deducted from prices. The German authorities came close to doing this in 1923, when they replaced the then reichmark with the rentenmark. They told their people a fable about the rentenmark being related to the land, but the effect of the change was to cut pay and prices. Unfortunately, this method also reduced savings in step, thereby preserving the injustice done to savers by inflation. It could then be seen that there was insufficient purchasing power in the economy and that inflation had reduced the quantities of basic and nominal money in real terms.

When the cost of increased pay is recouped from higher prices, employers have succeeded in passing on the additional expense to the public in general. As a result, savings have lost in value and an inequitable transfer of purchasing power has taken place from savers to workforces. It is important, therefore, that when pay is cut and prices reduced in order to cure inflation, savings should be left untouched, so as to effect a transfer of purchasing power in the reverse direction in compensation. The cure for inflation is the opposite of its cause.

It is equally important that deflation is not taken too far by excessive action in favour of the buyers. If that situation does arise, the correct remedy would be to increase pay and prices until the excess had been removed. The art is to achieve the equilibrium which allows for the buyers' disadvantages, that is, the weighted equilibrium.

We can also consider the inflation which took place in the Confederacy during the American Civil War. In that case, the blame has been placed on the authorities for printing money to finance expenditure.

First, let us refresh our memories on the principles of the processes by which basic money is created and destroyed. A unilateral transaction is impossible, so only the joint situation matters. In relation to the quantity of basic money, it is, in brief, as follows:

(a) Creditor spending on creditor services – no change.
(b) Debtor spending on debtor services – no change.
(c) Debtor spending on creditor services – an increase.
(d) Creditor spending on debtor services – a reduction.

This is the situation as it is today and it was exactly the same at the time of the Confederacy. Arguments based on the unilateral situation alone must inevitably be false, while those founded on the joint one should be correct. It has been assumed that the Confederate monetary authorities could create money on their own – a unilateral situation – whereas there had to be another party to each transaction they engaged in. A government or note-issuing authority is simply one of the participants in the market-place (one of the service debtors) and the same rules of basic money creation and destruction apply equally to all such parties.

If the sellers had insisted on charging stable prices to all buyers, including the government, inflation could not have arisen, even if the authorities printed extra notes to cover additional expenditure. It should be noted, too, that a government would not lose its power to create more basic money supply debts if the printing presses were in private hands. They could buy banknotes, just as we all do at present.

Governments under pressure or irresponsible ones may use the printing presses to facilitate the process by which they get themselves further into debt in terms of services. The presses may then become accomplices, but that does not make them the culprits or justify the notion that there is a monetary phenomenon.

Once one starts with the false premise that basic money can be created unilaterally, it is easy to conclude incorrectly that the printing of nominal money is the cause of inflation. Moreover, it leads to the further false conclusion that all modern forms of money are liabilities of financial institutions, instead of those of the service debtors.

Most of the Confederacy's expenditure would have been on debtor services, since the main suppliers would almost all have been borrowers, and would not have increased the quantity of basic money; to the extent that it did, it had to be on creditor services.

In inflationary conditions, all the participants in the market-place start charging one another more and an increase in the demand for cash from the issuing authorities results. It is wrong, therefore, to blame only one participant, in this case the Confederacy. Governments try to cover their expenditure by exacting higher taxes, increasing borrowing and selling assets.

Cash is the most convenient method of settling many transactions. The note issue, therefore, allows increased trading activity to take place, which in turn leads to a higher standard of living. That is what the printing press ensures. It is not a catalyst of inflation.

The Union army overran the location of the Confederacy's printing presses and the rate of inflation fell. It rose again when printing was resumed at a new site. From these events, it has been deduced that the printing of money – actually the printing of nominal money – is the cause of inflation.

Trade would have been hampered in these circumstances and the position of the sellers would have been weakened. All events simply assist the buyers or the sellers in the market-place and the rate of inflation or deflation is the natural reflection.

One has to look at the forces which were allowing prices to be pushed up. For example, in wartime profiteering arises and the Confederacy had to pay blockade runners to bring in essential items in short supply. There are no circumstances in which the printing can be the catalyst. Banknotes are printed in response to the demand for them and cash has no will of its own.

Let me clinch the matter. Suppose that in Great Britain the banks were merged into one, that the nation became cashless and that all transactions were settled through the new bank's computer. Cash would disappear and the printing presses could be dismantled.

Each party would only be allowed one account. Deposits would then represent the exact total holdings of basic money supply credits owned by the service creditors and advances the exact total amount of debts owned by the service debtors. Since the bank's own account would be included in advances, the two totals would balance.

The concept of broad money would be revealed as unsound and it would be clear that only the basic money supply exists. Payments from service debtors to service creditors would be seen to increase the basic money supply and those in the opposite direction to reduce it. The facts are undeniable.

There is, however, nothing in this system to stop employers granting pay increases and recouping the cost from higher prices. Inflation would be unimpeded. It is not caused by printing nominal money. Increases in the cost of services are the sole cause of inflation. The conditions in the Confederacy were not precisely the same as in this modern example, but the principles still applied.

Material wealth makes a party creditworthy and can be used in exchange, or as collateral, for a holding of the basic money supply. The owners of the gold and silver imported into Spain in the 16th century contributed nothing by that action to the economy in terms of services, but became creditworthy on account of their material wealth. They spent themselves into debt in terms of services, thereby increasing basic money supply debts and were charged over the odds for goods and services provided. The events were the triggers, but the ensuing inflation was caused by the general increase in pay and prices.

In the same way, it was the hourly increases in pay and prices which stoked up the rampant inflation in Germany in the early 1920s, while the growing quantity of cash and its continuous loss of value per unit were simply reflections.

Nowadays, when business activity is growing, inflation tends to rise on account of greed and, in the opposite circumstances, is apt to fall through fear of unemployment.

Making deductions from empirical evidence is clearly a very dangerous and inaccurate procedure. It is much safer and more logical to study the transactions taking place in modern economies.

The wages/prices spiral

Inflation is often said to be caused by the wages/prices spiral. One version of the argument holds that wage increases cause price increases, which lead to further wage increases and so on, while a second maintains that price increases are the catalysts in starting off the process. Basic money is created by debtor spending on creditor services and destroyed by creditor spending on debtor services. It follows that the action which comes first is the one which creates basic money and that, of course, is the payment of wages for work in progress.

Price increases can only affect inflation when they are paid, and they cannot be met unless there is enough basic money to cover them. If prices are raised unilaterally, fewer goods are sold. Suppliers are then forced to reduce prices, as they need to recover working capital through sales on a continuous basis to remain in business. Wage increases, therefore, cause price increases, because the additional cost has to be recouped. There is, however, no spiral. If further wage increases are not granted, additional price increases are not necessary and, in any event, could not be met. The spiral is a figment of the imagination and is used as an excuse in wage bargaining to justify more claims.

It is unsound to maintain that increases in wages are needed to keep up with, or ahead of, the cost of living, as the latter is comprised of payments to people, or, in other words, their remuneration. The argument has now become that wage increases are needed to keep up with, or ahead of, other people's wages. No one, therefore, requires a wage increase. Rising prices merely confirm that the workforce are being overpaid.

Avarice of management and aspirations of workers put upward pressure continuously on pay and prices, thereby giving the impression that there is an inevitable wages/prices spiral. A government which fails to counter these forces has lost the economic battle before it has begun.

Since business and industry agree higher pay levels and recoup the cost from increased prices, they are responsible for inflation. That is why inflation is largely a 20th century problem. Yet, management has escaped the blame!

At any given time, there is a pay and price level which the economy can support, and would probably allow full employment. It is irresponsible, therefore, to permit too high a pay and price level to be imposed on the economy. There is no way it can carry such a burden. Moreover, when the economy contracts, it becomes less and less able to support the existing level, far less a rising one.

Summing up, wage rises come before price increases. In consequence, the next wage rise has no valid connection with the last price increase. There seems to be a wages/prices spiral, but it is more apparent than real. The spiral is made up of pairs of separate incidents – each comprising a wage rise and a corresponding price increase – connected only by verbiage!

The true source of wage increases

When an inflationary wage increase is granted, more basic money is created while production remains at the same level. Prices are put up, but the services in which parties trade are unaltered. It is, therefore, the measure of these services which has been changed, and that alters the purchasing power of the basic money supply. This supply is debased or diluted rather than increased. As an analogy, it is similar to adding a pint of water to a gallon of milk and then claiming that there are nine pints of the beverage. Consequently, everyone owning part of the basic money supply credits has lost a little bit of purchasing power per pound.

The employers recoup the cost of the wage increase by putting up prices and the public is left to cope with the extra expense as best it can. Thus, instead of being a transfer of purchasing power from employers to employees, inflationary wage increases result in a transfer of purchasing power to the employees from the rest of the community, which includes the poor, the elderly, the unemployed, the sick, the disabled and other people on fixed incomes.

Workers often claim that they are being exploited. Now it transpires that, in inflationary conditions, they are doing the exploiting and their victims are the rest of the community. Increases in management remuneration have the same effect. The public, bemused by the myth of credit creation, is unaware that inequitable transfers of purchasing power are taking place.

It has become accepted that there has to be an annual round of wage increases, even when employers do not have the resources to meet them. They overcome this difficulty by arranging additional borrowing facilities with their banks. Then they raise prices to recoup the extra expenditure. The purchasing power of the pound is debased. Doubtless, it is not the intention of the parties involved to do precisely that, but equally there can be no denying that this is the effect.

There is nothing wrong in an employer who has the resources paying a wage increase, provided that prices are not raised to recoup it. Transfers of purchasing power in this way are not inflationary. The employer would be a service creditor owning deposits or a service debtor operating within a borrowing facility. Such a service debtor is able to pay the wage increase because he has first reduced his borrowing with earnings.

Most of the suppliers of goods and services are service debtors so basic money is only increased by payments from them to service creditors. Service debtor recipients have their indebtedness reduced at the expense of their employers, leaving basic money unchanged in amount.

These service debtors are within their overdraft limits. They can increase their borrowing again by spending or may be in a position to allow their indebtedness to remain reduced. If they take the first course of action, the extra purchasing power in the community will equal the wage increase, while if they settle for the second, they will make it easier for other parties to borrow. Either way, therefore, the extra purchasing power in the community will equal the additional wage payments in nominal terms. Employers can now raise prices to recoup the cost of the wage increase.

The rest of the community, however, has lost part of its purchasing power. Consequently, fewer goods and services will be sold and the economy will contract.

In inflationary conditions, borrowers repay their loans with ever depreciating currency. The result is that they are repaying less value in terms of services than obtained. Part of the basic money supply is wiped out unfairly by this process, thereby reducing the purchasing power in the community. Our addiction, at all levels, to pay increases is the cause of inflation and results in basic money being expressed in increasingly exaggerated terms. Thus, purchasing power in the economy is contracting, while it appears to be increasing. The process puts some people out of work and will continue to do so until remedial action is taken. Its effects are alleviated to some extent by scientific and technological advances, but those, in stable conditions, would produce a negative rate of inflation.

Such advances make it easier and cheaper on a continuous basis to meet the needs of the community and, in a properly managed economy, would reflect in falling prices. Then the benefits would be shared by all members of the community. Instead, workforces, in pursuit of a high wage economy and legitimate aspirations, have been allowed to acquire the benefits for themselves.

Governments have a blind spot in respect of the economy. They would not dream of allowing the roadway system to run without a highway code. Why should they believe that the economy does not need an equivalent?

An inflationary cycle?

At present, the rate of inflation rises and falls, so the impression is given that a cycle is inevitable. This is only the case because efficient action has not been taken to eliminate inflation.

What causes the variations? Pay increases, at all levels, added to prices cause the new basic money supply credits to have less purchasing power and debase the outstanding ones. There is then less purchasing power in the community to buy the current supply of goods and services. Service creditors lose part of their purchasing power and debts become less burdensome to an equal extent. Bankruptcies and liquidations result and some factories close. Borrowing demand and interest rates fall together, unemployment increases and recession sets in.

Pay demands begin to abate and the economy contracts until it reaches a viable level at the bottom of the cycle. It is, however, now composed solely of the surviving businesses and is catering for the community to a lesser extent.

From this base, with the benefit of scientific and technological advances, the economy starts to grow again. Nothing material, however, has changed, so once more pay and prices are pushed higher than the economy can support and the next recession begins. Thus, the economy is trapped between two factors: (1) greed, particularly at boardroom level, at the top of the cycle and (2) fear of unemployment at the bottom. Indeed, the pattern is one of unsustainable growth and recurring setbacks.

Since the economy is presently trapped in this pattern by the market forces, it is safe to forecast a recession when the monetary aggregates increase and a recovery when they slow down. It is quite wrong, however, to assume that any form of monetary growth is a catalyst of any kind; it is simply a reflection of our economic behaviour. In any event, why is so much time wasted in forecasting the state of the economy when its condition can be assured by efficient management of the pay and price structure?

The economy is not going to break out of the pattern on its own, so we require a pay and prices policy. Those features which damage it have to be dealt with, while the others must be allowed unimpeded progress. Moreover, the economy needs to be designed to meet the needs of people and not to conform with predetermined statistical targets.

Productivity

We are told that most wage increases are related to gains in productivity. If that is so, why have prices been put up? The employers should have been able to pay the increases from their own resources.

In most cases, additional remuneration is recouped from increased prices. Moreover, all the unproductive people insist on maintaining differentials or preserving parity with the productive ones. All and sundry must then have a wage increase. Increased productivity becomes a national disaster!

In any event, many of the increases in productivity are due to scientific and technological advances. These benefits should be passed on to the consumers by price reductions, which would result in more business; instead, they are being dissipated in higher remuneration, which prices firms and companies out of their markets.

A balance must be preserved. Thus, if increased productivity is to be rewarded by wage increases, reductions in it need to be matched by wage cuts.

Further fallacies

It is constantly repeated that inflation is caused by too much money chasing too few goods and services and that deflation occurs in the reverse circumstances. Experience in small markets can readily deceive us into believing that these contentions are correct. Now, however, we should realise that the criterion is actually the bias in the terms of trade favouring either the service debtors or the service creditors.

The view that a small amount of inflation is needed to stimulate the economy has gained widespread acceptance. Nevertheless, it is untrue, for inflation is always damaging and ensures that the economy underperforms.

It is widely believed that increases in trading activity cause the economy to 'overheat' and that this state of affairs results in inflation. There is nothing inevitable in the chain of events. Indeed, the belief merely emphasises the need for the economy to be managed. Inflation can always be eliminated or prevented.

Many people think that there cannot be much wrong with the economy when wages are rising faster than inflation. In these circumstances, the workforces are acquiring the benefits of scientific and technological advances for themselves. If all other things had no effect, percentage wage increases would equal the rate of inflation.

Comparability with other businesses on a global scale is one of the many excuses used for increasing pay, particularly for executives. Logic, however, demands that, in stable conditions, pay above the median should be reduced and that below it increased. In inflationary circumstances, pay and prices must be cut.

Government legislation on trade union activity and the effects of recession reduced the upward pressure for wage increases. Excessively disproportionate benefits have, however, been awarded to many executives by their peers. It is wrong to believe that such increases can only be criticised on the grounds of envy. Pay and price increases debase the currency. All remuneration is, therefore, the business of the government.

Even in a democratic country, wage negotiations cannot safely be left to industry and trade unions to agree. Indeed, it is ludicrous to believe that such negotiations will produce an efficient pay and price structure.

Countries have to take into account their trading positions and global wages. Accordingly, we need to reduce our pay and price structure by stages, until the recurring balance of payments deficits are eliminated and we have an adequate share of global industry. New jobs should, on balance, improve our trading position. Reliance on the market forces is a negative policy, when the need is for a positive one.

Since inflation is caused by activities outside the monetary and banking systems, it cannot be influenced or cured by irrelevant monetary measures. Examples of these are attempting to control the quantity of money, restricting lending in general and tampering with interest rates. Only a pay and prices policy can succeed.

Net inflation – Net deflation

The belief that inflation is everywhere and always a monetary phenomenon has led to it being treated as if it existed in isolation; thus, either an economy must suffer from inflation *or* deflation. The fact, however, is that both conditions always exist in economies and any result is a *net* one.

Putting the position succinctly, more pay for the same or comparatively less work creates inflation; less pay for the same or comparatively more work causes deflation. *Ceteris paribus*, people receiving pay increases in excess of the rate of inflation create further inflation and reduce the purchasing power of the pound; those whose pay is cut, remains the same or is increased by less than the rate of inflation cause deflation and increase the purchasing power of the pound. In emotional terms, the 'fat cats' are inflating, while the scrawny ones are deflating. Now we know why inflation is, to some extent, being held in check.

In a small market, 'too much money chasing too few goods' enables sellers *to alter the terms of trade* by raising prices, but over-production, on the other hand, obliges them to make reductions. Again, we can note that the situation is never one way only and that the experiences of parties differ.

The use of a monetary system cannot be the catalyst for all these contrary results. Surely, now, we can bury the monetary phenomenon.

7

Monetary and Economic Conditions, Theories and Policies

Control of the economy

It should now be clear that there are major differences between the teaching of the economic establishment and my findings. The main and comprehensive one is that the teaching is based on theoretical fallacies as to the nature of 'money', whereas my contentions are founded on proven facts. They lead to an entirely different conception of the ideal economy and how to achieve it.

In these circumstances, one might wonder how the economy works at all. The reason is that it is run by business and industry and applied monetary policies have been irrelevant. Thus, the success of the economy has rested on whether or not management made sound decisions. In the event, the economy has consistently, and sometimes grievously, underperformed.

Management has proved to be too concerned with personal gain and not always worthy of being trusted to act in the national interest. The result is that our real economic problems have been largely ignored and dangerous situations are arising. The government should, therefore, take real, instead of theoretical, control of the economy.

Monetary and economic conditions

We need to identify these more precisely than in the past and to distinguish between six different ones. Each is the opposite of one of the others, so they can be dealt with in pairs, namely, (1) Growth and Destruction, (2) Boom and Recession and (3) Inflation and Deflation.

(1) Growth and Destruction

The growth of basic money supply, as opposed to its dilution, is entirely healthy and should be encouraged. A town needs more basic money than a village, a city more than a town and a country more than a city. A large basic money supply in real terms is an indication of the industrialisation of the economy, the spread of education, the ability to trade and the existence of prosperity. Growth can only be achieved with an increase in the basic money supply in real terms, so we must disabuse ourselves of the notion that inflation automatically follows. It does not do so and can only come from increases in remuneration being recouped from higher prices.

In certain circumstances basic money supply can be destroyed without being spent. A gift from a service creditor to a service debtor does this, but that is of little account, since such presents made in the opposite direction increase the basic money supply. Our concern is with major events, such as the liquidation of a large company, the collapse of a bank, an oil crisis, a food scare or the loss of a war. All eliminate part of the basic money supply or reduce its purchasing power, a situation which I have chosen to describe as 'Destruction'.

Recession, slump and depression are three words used to classify falls in economic activity. It is desirable, however, that a distinction should be made between the effects of a loss of basic money supply (destruction) and the results of parties refraining from spending (recession). In the first case, basic money supply has been reduced, while in the second it may be building up.

Looking back in time, the Great Depression in the United States was triggered by a truly major loss of basic money supply, which was only restored when the government of that country spent massive sums of borrowed funds in financing its participation in the Second World War.

(2) Boom and Recession

Booms cannot be sustained. Most of the suppliers of goods and services are service debtors and, in a boom, creditor spending rapidly reduces the basic money supply. It cannot be built up fast enough by the performance of creditor services for service debtors, so booms have to peter out.

Parties may be performing services as usual, but refraining as far as possible from spending their remuneration. As the basic money supply builds up, the suppliers make some price reductions to induce sales. The will to refrain from spending weakens and the recession ends.

The setback in Britain in the early 1990s was inadequately described as a recession, when it was, in fact, caused by major losses of basic money supply due to bad management decisions. It is an example of destruction. Parties refrained from spending, not from choice, but because they had lost purchasing power.

(3) Inflation and Deflation

These have already been dealt with. One point, however, falls to be emphasised.

In inflationary conditions, it is often contended that more money is chasing the same amount of goods and services, as a result of which prices rise. In fact, basic money supply has been diluted by pay and price increases and has not increased in real terms. We can, therefore, describe the position precisely. Thus, the same amount of basic money, now expressed in units of lesser value, is chasing the same amount of goods and services, now priced in the debased units. Some job losses would result, so eventually a slightly smaller amount of basic money, now expressed in more units of lesser value, would be chasing a slightly smaller amount of goods and services, now priced in the debased units. Inflation continuously destroys part of the basic money supply.

Monetary and economic theories

The economic establishment defines 'money as anything which acts as a medium of exchange, a unit of account or a store of value. Thus, they fail to distinguish between basic and nominal money. There is no mention in their teaching of the facts that (1) basic money is subject to a process of continuous creation and destruction and (2) the passing from hand to hand of media of exchange has different effects. Theories based on so inadequate a foundation must inevitably be unsound.

Before the last recession began, the monetary authorities were maintaining that credit was excessive, that the economy was overheating and that too much money was chasing too few goods and services. Accordingly, they raised interest rates in the belief that this would reduce demand and relieve inflationary pressures. This analysis was incorrect.

The notion that credit can be excessive stems from the mistaken belief that the banks create money by lending. In fact, basic money can only be created by debtor spending on creditor services. Borrowing should not be curbed and the deposits available for lending should be fully utilised. Credit can never be excessive; it is a limited resource.

Demand is financed by borrowing, but increases in it need not cause overheating or inflationary pressures. After all, lowering prices is the best way to stimulate demand. In any event, the higher the trading activity is, the better will be the standard of living. It is quite wrong, therefore, to try to contract or constrain the economy.

In developed countries, the expectations of the people grow constantly. These expectations have to be financed and that causes the ratio of borrowing to deposits to reach its upper limits. The problem is, therefore, not how to contract or constrain the economy, but how to make the available resources go further. Thus, demand should be accommodated, unless this can only be done at the expense of more desirable lending.

Savings always equal borrowings and the supply of goods and services is geared to anticipated purchasing power. It follows that the right amount of basic money should be chasing the correct quantity of goods and services. Consequently, if supply is increased or reduced, the creation of basic money will be similarly affected to the same extent. This equilibrium can only be disturbed by management mistakes and greed.

The expression of alternative views seems to have no effect on the monetary authorities. Here, for example, is an extract from my letter of 21 October 1989, published in the Winter edition that year by *Britain & Overseas*, the magazine of The Economic Research Council:

> Can the present high interest rate policy succeed? Sadly to say, it can only 'succeed', if it puts people out of work, reduces the standard of living and causes fewer goods and services to be financed by borrowing. Thus, it is a primitive way of reducing borrowing in relation to savings. It will cause a considerable contraction in the economy, damage and destroy businesses unnecessarily, penalise many people unfairly and cause us to lose further ground to our industrial competitors. Moreover, there is no knowing just how high interest rates will have to go to achieve these undesirable ends.

The assumption of the monetary authorities, as already noted, was that the high interest rates would reduce demand and relieve inflationary pressures. They sought to allow the economy to proceed at a more sedate pace. It did not seem to occur to them that curbing the economy ensures that it underperforms; moreover, they failed to realise that remedies in specific areas were required and not the blunt instrument of blanket coverage. The cost of financing the basic essential features of the standard of living was needlessly increased. Worse still, the authorities had abandoned, as a matter of politics, the correct way to deal with inflationary pressures, which is to cut pay and prices. Instead, they placed their faith in ineffective monetarism.

At the time, I shared the assumption that the high interest rates would reduce the demand for borrowing and my prediction of the results seemed subsequently to prove this view to be correct.

I have to confess, however, that I got the prediction right for the wrong reason. The raising of the interest rates proved ineffective and was not the catalyst of the setback. It transpired that the borrowers were little concerned with what interest rates they paid, because they believed that the sectors of the economy in which they were operating – property, insurance and banking – would continue to provide high profits.

The result was a classic example of what happens when too much borrowed money is thrown at specific markets. Unsustainable booms in those areas were generated. At their peaks, the buyers began to disappear and the markets collapsed. The sellers were unable to repay their borrowing; they had, in the chase after profits, built too much property, entered into unsound insurance contracts and engaged in imprudent lending. A major loss of basic money resulted and an equal amount of service credits and service debts was wiped out. The domino effect forced the economy to contract in much the same way, though perhaps more violently, as it would have done if the high interest rates had been effective.

Unfortunately, the monetary authorities have not learned the lesson and still believe that interest rate policy works.

Monetarism, on which the authorities have relied, is based on questionable conclusions drawn from a study of empirical evidence. This can lead to events having to take place, such as the runaway housing market, before action can be considered, far less taken. Thus, it is not suitable for modern economies, which need rapid responses when they start to go off course.

Monetarists claim that money, once created, has to be held and, moreover, that its quantity, calculated from monetary aggregates, can influence the behaviour of the economy. They could just not be more wrong. In truth, as we now know, it is nominal money which 'circulates' and, in the course of its passing, basic money is created and destroyed in accordance with the status rules. Basic money is the result of the trading activity and its outstanding quantity does not influence the behaviour of the economy. Such money has no will of its own and, consequently, is entirely neutral.

Unilateral monetary theory is a compilation of erudite opinions built up over the centuries. Unfortunately, they are based on an incorrect view of the nature of 'money'. The result is that the whole subject is unsound. In reality, owing to the accuracy of the monetary, banking and settlement systems, we get exactly the economy our collective behaviour warrants.

If official tampering with interest rates, or any other monetary measure, were effective in a helpful sense, it would have some merit. Nevertheless, it would still, at best, be a sneaky way of altering human behaviour, just as open and honest incomes policy does, or, more appropriately, a pay and prices policy would. Since, however, monetary measures simply tamper with the reflections of that behaviour, instead of the real thing, they inevitably fail.

Perhaps now the so-called monetarist golden age will be seen for what it really is – an age of folly. Moreover, the monetary authorities might realise that there really is no viable alternative to some form of pay and prices policy.

In the meantime, we can only trust that business and industry will perform more efficiently and with greater responsibility. As already noted, they run the economy. Consequently, the putting of their own houses more in order would improve our economic conditions. They could begin by cutting the excessive remuneration awarded to their executives and taking the savings from prices. In fairness, they have improved their performance since the recession. That said, however, there is little evidence to indicate that the leopard really has changed its spots or learnt the lesson of the setback.

Monetary and economic policies

The extent to which the monetary authorities are committed to theoretical policies should be fully appreciated. The Bank of England published a paper entitled 'The Interest Rate Transmission Mechanism'. *Inter alia*, it states, 'Concern has been expressed that deregulation may have weakened the mechanism through which monetary policy – meaning here interest rates – affects demand and inflation'. Moreover, it mentions that the government of the United Kingdom is committed to the use of such monetary policy in pursuing price stability.

A further contention is that, 'There are three broad mechanisms through which interest rates might operate; the cost of borrowing, the effects on incomes and wealth and the exchange rate'.

Notice the use of the word, 'might'.

Some objections to such theoretical monetary policies are:

(a) They are based on false conceptions as to the nature of 'money' and the way the economy works.

(b) They make no attempt to ensure that the benefits of scientific and technological advances are shared by all members of the public.

(c) They have proved to be of no help to the poor and the long-term unemployed. The gap between the rich and the poor continues to grow and, while good jobs are being lost, the replacements and additions have been mainly in the lowest paid sectors of the economy. Often, too, they are only part-time.

(d) They are given the credit for low rates of inflation, when fear of unemployment is the determining factor.

(e) Their objectives are inadequate. Thus, the Bank of England's quarterly report issued in May 1995 states that the challenge for monetary policy is to ensure that the cyclical upturn in inflation is modest! Inflation must be eliminated, not preserved.

(f) Their failure to eliminate inflation means that the economy always underperforms. We are unable to generate enough funds to finance our inventions, to carry out sufficient research and to improve health and other facilities.

(g) They are based on a pathological fear of inflation, when a pay and prices policy would eliminate it immediately and permanently.

(h) They have distracted attention from the need to deal with adverse practices in the market-place. Thus, executive pay has been allowed to be increased excessively and the housing market was permitted to run riot.

(i) They ignore the fact that the funds available for lending have become very important. The paramount needs now are, firstly, to protect them from misuse and, secondly, to ensure that they increase in value.

(j) They are negative and defensive by nature, when the economy should be encouraged to move forward, so that it takes better care of the nation as a whole.

(k) They are not aimed at our real problems.

Our real problems

These are, given our world-wide commitments, (a) an inadequate share of global industry, (b) recurring trade deficits, (c) considerable unemployment, (d) too high a pay and price structure and (e) excessive disparities between shopfloor and boardroom rewards.

(a) Global Industry

We need an adequate share of global industry, whether in manufacturing or services, so that we can trade at least in balance if not in credit. It is wrong to believe that, as a developed country, we can safely move into knowledge intensive industries and ignore traditional ones. The same economic forces will operate against us in these new industries as have in those we have lost or are losing. If we cannot protect a given industry, none will be safe.

Trade is not conducted on a level playing field. The Americans have a huge advantage from the interest-free loans they get from having a reserve currency, just as we once did. This is countered to some extent by their assumption of international responsibilities and their spending on them. Any trade disadvantage to us, however, must be offset by a lower pay and price structure. Comparability of financial rewards internationally is not an acceptable basis for increasing pay.

(b) Trade Deficits

It has been said that countries, unlike businesses, cannot go bankrupt and this contention was advanced in support of sovereign lending. True, there is no legal process to enforce the condition, but any nation which cannot pay its international debts, is insolvent in fact, if not in law.

Countries which trade continuously at a loss are verging on insolvency, so the balance of payments is an important issue. Trade deficits cannot be financed indefinitely and have to be settled. This is done by the home debtors realising foreign assets or by foreign creditors accepting payment in sterling in London. That sterling is then used to purchase home assets or to set up foreign-owned businesses in this country. To describe these practices as inward investment is a euphemism. The collective experience is not unlike that of the bankrupt, who has some of his assets seized by the bailiffs!

As we have noted, sterling balances do not leave the country because we have our own currency. Continuing trade deficits, however, result in more of them being owned by foreigners. These balances, whether home- or foreign-owned, are lent overnight on the London money market, so the damage being done does not show up there.

Transactions in sterling between foreigners are settled by exchanges in their own currencies held abroad. Danger arises when foreign sellers of sterling are offered falling rates of exchange by foreign buyers, thus devaluing our currency.

It is wrong to believe that we can safely cover our recurring trade deficits permanently by continually borrowing foreign currency. Bankrupts should not be encouraged to increase their debts! Equally, sterling cannot be defended, except in the very short term, by raising interest rates to make the balances more attractive for the foreigners to hold. This is a very damaging practice, to which resort should never be made. The proper function of the interest rates is to hold the ring between the demand for borrowing and the supply of deposits available for lending.

Owing to the trade deficits, the failure to offset the damage done by inflation and the weakness of sterling, Britain became one of the lower wage industrialised countries in the European Union. This made it attractive to foreign companies wishing to achieve access to the common market. Such inward investment, however, owes no allegiance to this country and, when the European Union is expanded eastwards, may well be moved to the lower wage industrialised economies there. The effects could be devastating.

(c) Unemployment

Full employment is not a dream; it is the natural state of affairs. In primitive societies, all the adults and many of the children contribute to the wellbeing of the tribe and, in totalitarian ones, people can be directed into work. Since such societies can achieve full employment, it should also be within the reach of free nations.

Many governments have abandoned the notion that full employment can be obtained. They have done so, however, without an adequate knowledge of how economies work. Clearly, with better policies more jobs would become available, so that must be the objective. The government needs to take control of the economy from business and industry and bring the gift of employment within its powers.

A command economy, such as a communist one, is not being advocated. It is just that the economy has to be made to observe certain parameters, within which business and industry could operate more efficiently. The factors which damage the economy and have led to our relative decline would be removed.

Consider the root cause of unemployment. All charges are made by people, acting as individuals or in concert, and every payment goes to them in one capacity or another. Consequently, all costs, however described, are payments for services, productive or otherwise. Increases in any of them, when recouped from prices, debase the currency, reduce the value of savings, bankrupt weaker businesses and cause unemployment. Thus, the insistence of the workforces, at all levels, in pushing up pay and prices is the root cause of unemployment. Everyone who does not perform services, for whatever reason, has to be supported by the workforces. It is folly, therefore, on their part to price people out of work and to prevent them from obtaining jobs because labour is too expensive. Fortunately, a pay and prices policy could reverse these undesirable features.

It has been said that scientific and technological advances cause unemployment by making some people redundant. This is true, but it is only one side of the coin. Such advances create additional industries and new occupations, so there does not have to be an effect adverse to employment.

Many people believe that jobs can be created by spending, but, in modern conditions, this is not the case. The funds available for lending tend to be fully utilised and any allocated for new investment can only be obtained by diverting some from their existing uses. New investment then replaces old and jobs created are offset by jobs destroyed, a current example of which has been more employment in services and less in manufacturing.

The formation of new companies and the liquidation of old ones are both at or near record levels. Unemployment remains high, though for the past three years – 1994 to 1996 – the trend has been slowly downwards. Thus, investment on a large scale is already taking place and those are the results. More spending will not change them.

When, before the Second World War, public expenditure was advocated to reduce unemployment, the funds available for lending were underused and some could be borrowed without disturbing the low interest rates. It was a sound proposition then, as would have been more hire purchase and mortgage loans; it is not an available remedy now.

In these circumstances, it would be tragic for the unemployed if more funds were spent in further fruitless efforts, however well intentioned, to come to their aid.

That, however, does not mean that the problem should be shelved as unsolvable. On the contrary, a government which claims to care should recognise that policies not aimed at full employment are both cruel and unnecessary. Economic advisers should, therefore, be instructed to devise policies to reduce unemployment more effectively.

(d) The Pay and Price Structure

Because the way in which the economy works has not been understood, the accepted opinion has been that if all parties work for their own interests, the most efficient economy will result. Now that the facts are known, it is clear that this principle can only work if parties know where their best interests lie. In any event, consideration for the interests of others is what is actually required.

The benefits of scientific and technological advances should in themselves produce a negative rate of inflation. Thus, even the poorest parties in our society should continually gain purchasing power. As things are, however, they are being cheated out of their share. In witness, it was reported in February 1996 that if the £10

Christmas bonus paid to pensioners had been index-linked, its value in that month would have been £67.

Pay increases, including perquisites, recouped from prices are, of course, the culprits. In these circumstances, perhaps even the most deserving groups will withdraw their pay claims and managements will accept the need to cut remuneration, not at the bottom, but progressively thereafter. The savings in costs would fall to be deducted from prices.

It is unrealistic to believe that a sound pay and price structure will result from agreements between employers and employees or that managements can help themselves to limitless rewards. The controlling feature must be the state of trade or, in other words, the balance of payments. Countries trading at a loss should cut pay and prices. This principle applies to all economies, whether advanced, developing, stagnant or backward.

(e) Shopfloor and Boardroom Rewards
The trade unions were wrong to chase after a high wage economy. The paradox is that, as already noted, the resulting inflation and loss of jobs has caused the British economy to be one of the lower wage ones of the industrialised countries in the European Union. Part of the basic money supply has been continuously destroyed and the economy has consistently underperformed. Instead of trying to keep up, the unions should have insisted on the higher salaries and perquisites being clawed back. One man does not need one hundred times or more remuneration than another in the same business. The excessive disparities between shopfloor and boardroom rewards should be reduced.

Since the pay and price structure cannot be left safely to employers and employees, the government should recognise that it has a duty to control it with an earnings policy.

The recession

The failure and irrelevance of monetary policy made the recession of the early 1990s inevitable, as nothing was done to prevent it. Thus, as events developed, the annual round of pay increases added to prices, coupled with bad management decisions, overwhelmed the economy. As we have seen, that combination resulted in major financial losses, particularly in property, insurance and banking. The ensuing bankruptcies and liquidations destroyed part of the basic money supply, the capacity to trade and the ability to create new funds. The economy was forced to contract and was left with insufficient purchasing power to maintain the standard of living. Moreover, associated businesses were brought down by the knock-on effects, unemployment increased and the rate of inflation fell without any help from the monetary authorities.

Ineffective monetary measures failed to prevent inflation arising in the first place and should not be credited with causing the subsequent falls in its rate. Thus, it is quite wrong to believe that it was the high interest rates which brought inflation down from $9^{1}/_{2}$ per cent in 1990 to little more than $2^{1}/_{2}$ per cent in 1995. The catalyst was a reduction in the pay claims of workforces living in fear of unemployment.

Three groups could have prevented the recession, (1) the employers, (2) the banks and (3) the government.

(1) When the recession began, employers chose to release surplus employees onto the labour market. Yet they could instead have cut all remuneration and kept up the level of business by taking the savings in costs from prices. Employees should be given the chance to save their jobs.

(2) Inflation has a weakness; it has to be financed. Consequently, most pay increases require bank borrowing. Thus, the employers do not pay them from their own resources. Prudent banks should, therefore, provide finance for additional business, but not for pay increases. One might, of course, feel that the Bank of England, as the regulatory authority, should have issued instructions along these lines. What better answer to an inflationary pay claim could the employers have than that the banks would not finance it?

(3) The government could eliminate inflation overnight. All it has to do is, by law, to oblige employers to cut all forms of remuneration and take the savings in costs from prices.

Since inflation can be cured and prevented by any of the foregoing proposals, or variants of them, it cannot be a monetary problem or phenomenon. Readers might like to note that they tip the scales in favour of the buyers in the market-place. It has been said that there is no way in which inflation can be brought down without reductions in demand and spending. Clearly, now, that view is untenable; there are several ways.

Here is an extract from another of my letters. This one was dated 7 June 1992 and published in the Summer edition that year of *Britain & Overseas*.

> There is no economic cycle – only periods of good and bad management decisions. The worst ones have been made by countries most affected by recessions. Recovery is not, therefore, assured. Indeed, our own recession will probably deepen, as more major losses keep coming to light.

In an effort to survive the recession, business and industry reorganised their structures, sold non-core activities, put more emphasis on exports, dispensed with some employees and offered unsustainable discounts.

These last-ditch practices have given the impression that recovery is taking place. Nothing, however, has been done to cure our real problems. Consequently, the features that caused the recession are still largely in place and, unless remedial action is taken, could well prompt a fresh bout of inflation and yet another setback.

Financing inflation

Inflation can be financed by employers obtaining extra cash for the payment of wage increases.

The commercial banks maintain accounts with the Bank of England. These accounts have to be maintained in credit at or above stipulated levels at the end of each business day and more banknotes are obtained at their debit.

As a result, the Banking Department becomes short of cash and, to remedy this situation, replenishes its holding by obtaining further supplies from the Issue Department in exchange for government securities.

The commercial banks lend their surplus cash to the discount houses overnight rather than keep it in their Bank of England accounts. Withdrawals of notes reduce the total sums available for this purpose and the banks call in the deficits from the discount houses.

On the basis that all other things are equal in the meantime, the houses are obliged to inform the Bank of England that they are short of funds and are normally given assistance. Thus, the Bank may buy government securities, mainly Treasury Bills, from the houses or grant them temporary overdraft facilities. Either way, the funds made available are paid to the commercial banks and are used to restore the balances of their accounts.

Distribution of the notes to the appropriate bank branches then takes place and the employers draw them to pay the wage increases. The recipients are now able to spend more and, when they do, the notes pass into the hands of shopkeepers, who pay them back into the local bank branches. There they are held for reissue on the next pay day, with the exception of those which have to be replaced, such as soiled or mutilated ones. Some of the cash may not, of course, be spent and, if deposited with banks, could drift back to the Bank of England as funds surplus to requirements. However, in the main, notes covering wage increases remain in circulation or, rather, outstanding.

The net result of the transactions is that the Bank of England has obtained government securities to the value of the extra notes. Thus, assets have been acquired and cash issued. The quantity of nominal money is now relatively greater than the total prices of the goods and services on sale. Employers can, therefore, raise their prices and recoup the cost of the wage increases. The inflationary process is complete.

Assume that total purchasing power in the community was £2,970 million when wage increases of £30 million were granted. The new total is, therefore, £3,000 million. If we express the position in real terms on a 'before and after' basis, we arrive at the following comparison:

	Total Purchasing Power		Real Terms
Before	2,970,000,000 × £1	=	£2,970,000,000
After	3,000,000,000 × 99p	=	£2,970,000,000

The purchasing power of the pound has fallen by 1 per cent and £30 million is, of course, 1 per cent of £3,000 million.

Increases in notes in circulation give the impression that the Bank of England is increasing the basic money supply. These media of exchange, however, are nominal, and not basic, money. When they are drawn (bought) by the commercial banks from the Bank of England and issued to their branches, the movements are redispositions. The act of increasing the basic money supply occurs when service debtor employers pay wage increases to service creditor employees.

Closer examination of the situation shows, of course, that the basic money supply has been diluted rather than increased. Thus, every party holding part of it has given up a little bit of purchasing power to the employees.

It was noted that when cash moves from the Bank of England to the commercial banks, government securities of equivalent value normally flow from the discount houses to that institution. The converse is also true. Thus, when cash goes from the commercial banks to the Bank of England, government securities of equivalent value usually flow from the central bank to the discount houses. The principles apply to all payments, and not just to cash ones, between the commercial banks and the Bank of England. The houses and the central bank are service debtors, so transactions between them have no effect on total basic money supply.

The much vaunted open market operations must be brought into perspective against the background of how basic money is created and destroyed. Consequently, in the overall picture, open market operations are comparatively minor dealings taking place within the direct investment status rules. Most gilt-edged securities are never far from their issue prices.

On the occasions when the Bank of England grants overdraft facilities to the discount houses, the practice is a temporary expediency intended to tide them over situations which are expected to correct themselves rapidly, often on the following business day. This form of assistance, although important in itself, should be looked on as a comparatively minor exception to the rule that government securities pass between the discount houses and the Bank of England in the opposite direction to cash, and other payments, moving between the commercial banks and the central one.

The commercial banks can also finance inflation by granting additional lending facilities to their customers to cover increases in wage payments made by cheque or credit to accounts. Employers are then able to recoup the cost by raising prices.

The Bank of England borrows all the funds deposited with it, except its cash holding, and uses them for lending, investment, etc. Thus, it acts in the same fashion as the commercial banks and pushes basic money in dormant situations back into use. Redisposed funds flowing into the hands of the monetary authorities do not reduce the basic money supply nor does their movement in the opposite direction increase it.

When the central bank takes Special Deposits, it releases the basic money supply they represent if it uses the funds in the normal way. The practice then becomes completely ineffective, which is fortunate.

Basic money flows through the banking system, the parts of which are interconnected. We may talk of private and public sectors, but basic money simply does not recognise them. The monetary authorities are participants in the market-place, just like any other party and the system is separate from the transactions it settles. Those involving the monetary authorities as one of the parties rather than as operators of part of the Pool affect the basic money supply outside the banking system in accordance with the status rules. There are no exceptions. In the banking system, democracy rules! The Bank of England's operations have, therefore, no more effect on inflation than those of any other participants in the banking system.

We have noted that the Bank mops up surplus funds in, and provides assistance to, the money market as the need arises. In addition, it accommodates the transactions of its own customers – mainly banks and government departments – in the same way as the commercial banks look after theirs. Making the system work is the essence of banking. In respect of its transactions, the Bank should be seen as an integral, effective and necessary part of the system and not as an authority supposedly endowed with powers to manipulate the basic money supply. It cannot be said too often; parties trade in services. There is nothing a central bank, relying on monetary policy, can do about that.

To exercise control over the economy, the Bank of England would need extra powers and be willing to use them. In the main, such powers would enable it (1) to cut pay and prices to repair damage done by inflation and (2) to prevent inflation being financed.

Demand accommodation

It is pointless to ask the thrifty to save more. Savings always equal borrowings. Thus, the spenders are being asked to borrow more! This shows up the folly of the tax relief being granted under the Peps and Tessa schemes, on the one hand, and on mortgage loans on the other. The way forward is to make the funds available for lending more valuable.

The extent to which the economy is off course must first be recognised. The constant rounds of remuneration increases continually destroy equal parts of the outstanding service credits and service debts or, in short, the basic money supply. This leads to a lopsided economy, in which the fittest and the favoured can readily live in comfort while others suffer deprivation.

Modern economies are completely dependent on credit, that is, the funds available for lending. Wages and salaries are paid in advance; our purchases of goods and services are financed before we pay for them; and credit is extended even further in respect of mortgage loans and hire purchase ones. The simple truth is that remuneration increases are incompatible with this situation. Therefore, the avarice of managements and the aspirations of the workers have to be met by price reductions and not pay increases; these reductions would arise from the benefits of scientific and technological advances.

At any given time, there is a remuneration level which the economy can support and around which our current difficulties would disappear. The first action necessary is, therefore, to bring the present pay level down to the supportable one by cutting all remuneration and insisting on the savings in costs being deducted from prices. The workforces would have lower incomes, but goods would be cheaper to buy, so the remedy would not be painful. If it were hurting it would *not* be working! Moreover, the subsequent rewards would make it well worthwhile.

The workforces would share the benefits of scientific and technological advances, which would show up in prices falling faster than pay. People on fixed incomes would find that their purchasing power was steadily increasing. The poor, too, would share this experience, which is a matter of great importance. More jobs would result.

As the members of the present workforces retire, they would enjoy the aforementioned benefits and would not be faced with the misery of being cheated by inflationary practices, as the present generation of pensioners have been. Inflation creates poverty; deflation can lead to a general improvement in living standards.

A reduction in the rate of inflation should not be described as deflation. The correct term is, 'disinflation', and the result is that inflation is being preserved at lower levels. Deflation eliminates inflation.

Care, too, must be exercised in the use of the word 'demand'. In the context of this book, it means the ability to pay for requirements and does not include need, which cannot be financed. It is anticipated that as the general level of prosperity rises, the poor would gain purchasing power and need would be converted to demand. This is a very different economy from any we have so far achieved.

Because it has wrongly been accepted that increased trading activity inevitably results in inflation, all forms of monetary policy are designed to curb the economy. Demand management and monetarism are the two leading examples of this unsound philosophy, but every bit as damaging is the notion that interest rates should be manipulated – 'the interest rate transmission mechanism' – to curb and encourage the economy. All these are negative policies and must be replaced with positive ones. We have to move to the more advanced principle of demand accommodation, financed by the increasing purchasing power of the funds available for lending.

It is simply not possible to manage, and drive forward, a modern economy efficiently without some form of pay and prices policy. To some extent, therefore, the professors who advocated incomes policy were on the right lines, but only in so far as it related to pay and prices. Where have they all gone?

Workforces, too, have been their own worst enemies in asking for pay increases. They should have demanded that the higher levels of pay be clawed back, rather than have allowed their own standards of living to fall relatively in a fruitless effort to keep up.

Every developed country comes up against the barrier created by the ratio of borrowing to deposits at the top. Our economy hits it more often than our industrial competitors, because of the addiction to larger pay increases. Additional trading activity causes an equal, though net, increase in deposits and advances and that alone raises the ratio of borrowing to deposits, even without the extensive damage done by pay increases. The benefits of the free market system are being nullified and it is alarming to consider the pressure additional government borrowing could create by 'crowding out' other lending.

8

Remedial Measures

The state of the economy

The real problems of the country were discussed in the previous chapter. As noted, they are not being addressed and, as a result, dangerous situations could arise.

Membership of the European Union has not delivered the antici-pated benefits and the associated economies are being outperformed by many of those in the Far East. Combining ill-run economies will not produce an efficient conglomerate, so we must put our own house in order before the folly of the bureaucrats becomes unstoppable.

The economics profession has gone terribly wrong in attributing the nature of basic money (credits and debts in services) to the titles (media of exchange). Moreover, they have failed to determine how basic money is created and ignored the ways in which it is destroyed. In consequence, their versions of monetary theory – the unilateral kind – are almost entirely unsound.

Monetary policy, where effective, can only be damaging, as it interferes with a very efficient settlement system. For the most part, however, it has been irrelevant, as it does not bear on our real problems. Exchange rates and interest rates are not levers by which the economy can be manipulated, but simply reflections of its condition. Thus, attempts to maintain an artificial exchange rate must inevitably fail; devaluation merely recognises a situation which already exists, while leaving the causes in place to force another one; and official tampering with interest rates transfers purchasing power unfairly between service creditors and service debtors, according to which group it favours.

The quantity of basic money is the net result of the processes of continuous creation and destruction. In consequence, it, too, is a reflection of the state of the economy, and not a catalyst which can influence it.

For these reasons, the pay and price level is the key to the economy and the only lever by which it can be managed. Accordingly, successful economic measures have to affect human behaviour and not its reflections.

Scientific and technological advances should ensure that prices fall slightly each year. This does not happen in our country, because chairmen, directors, managers and the rest of the workforces take too much from their companies. Thus, they have excessive remuneration, golden handshakes, stock options, profit-sharing, company cars, assisted mortgage loans, private health cover, subsidised dining rooms, luncheon vouchers, annual wage and salary increments, higher rates for overtime and unsociable hours, dirty and danger money, etc. Nearly all the costs of these rewards have to be financed by bank borrowing and set the standards by which the professions and other workforces expect to be remunerated. Personally, I feel that stock options are morally wrong. Executives should be prepared to give their best efforts in return for their salaries.

We have already noted the factors which destroyed a large part of our basic money supply, caused the recession, forced the economy to contract, brought down the rate of inflation and left the economy with insufficient purchasing power to maintain the standard of living, plus the contributory one of the Treasury's ill-fated attempt to prevent the pound falling through its lower limit in the Exchange Rate Mechanism.

Nothing of much consequence has changed, so only slow recovery is happening at present. The lost basic money supply cannot be replaced overnight. Nevertheless, the value of the remainder could be increased by pay and price cuts, thereby making good the deficiency. New basic money being created would then have more purchasing power per pound than the outstanding amount and would cause the latter to increase in value in step. Demand would increase without inflation and more jobs would become available. No other remedy can produce these results.

For example, recovery cannot be obtained by (1) investment, for there is only enough basic money to finance and purchase the current supply of goods and services; (2) taxation and redistribution of income, as that merely transfers purchasing power; (3) restricting credit and bank lending, since that puts difficulties in the way of desirable trade; or (4) containing inflation or lowering its annual rate of increase, as that preserves the problem in varying degrees. No, the currency must be refined, and that translates into reducing all remuneration. More work must be done for less basic money.

Economic recovery must be kept in perspective. Thus, we must not aim for the vastly overextended positions at the height of the last boom, but, on the other hand, we must not set our sights too low. The correct remedial measures would ensure steady growth without inflation and it might become clear, in the not too distant future, that the pre-war rate of US\$4.50 to £1 might not be out of reach. That, after all, represents the extent in real terms to which we have fallen behind.

No matter how we twist and turn, it becomes steadily more obvious that only a pay and prices policy is a practicable economic measure. Let us not, therefore, hear any defeatist talk to the effect that one cannot be introduced. The state of the economy makes it essential.

The supportable pay and price level

As already mentioned, there is, at any given time, a pay and price level which would result in the absence of inflation or deflation. This can be described as 'the supportable level'.

If the pay and price level is above the supportable one, the currency will lose purchasing power and considerable unemployment will result; this adverse state of employment may, however, be hidden to some extent by good full-time jobs being replaced by low-paid and part-time ones.

On the other hand, if the pay and price level is below the supportable one, the currency will gain in purchasing power and more jobs will become available.

The existing pay and price level can be pushed towards the supportable one, but the converse is not also the case. Obviously, attempting to find the exact supportable level would be too ambitious, so 'the area of tolerance' on either side of it must be the objective.

To this end, we must begin by introducing remedial measures which favour the service creditors at the expense of the service debtors. This is only fair, as the latter have been allowed to cheat the former for too long.

The two phases of the remedial measures

A pay and prices policy, consisting of two phases, is required. The purpose of the first is to push the existing pay and price level down to the area of tolerance and, of the second, to hold it there.

Translating this theoretical concept into practice, the first phase is needed to repair the damage done by compounding inflation, to offset the loss of basic money supply, to obtain an adequate share of global industry, to eliminate the recurring trade deficits and to reduce unemployment substantially. It would consist of a series of pay and price cuts of whatever number and to whatever extent proved necessary to achieve these objectives. The effects on our real problems can now be considered.

(a) Global Industry
The effects of the pay and price cuts would make it possible for us to regenerate marginal global industries, which we have lost, and to move the rest higher above the danger levels. They would also deter the occasional practice of British industry of transferring production to lower wage economies abroad.

These principles apply also to small businesses, which might make the difference between them being a drag on the economy, through failures, or a contributory factor to it, from growth. It was reported in 1996 that 80 per cent of them have no export trade, so their place in the economy must be kept in perspective. They are only a small part of the global position.

The major benefits would probably show up in the City of London. Sterling would appreciate, but not to the full extent, as all our activities do not involve international trade. It could become a reserve currency again and a formidable case might develop for the European central bank to be sited in London. That could be the prize for being the first country to demonstrate how a modern economy should be managed. I am of the opinion that the countries in the European Union should retain their own currencies to prevent their funds available for lending moving to the home of a single currency. Some of them, however, could find it advantageous to conduct their foreign trade in sterling. There is no need for the euro. Being at the centre of the European Union geographically, Germany will always have strong industry; Britain, I believe, should have the financial aspects.

(b) Trade Deficits
Our exports would become cheaper, but not to the full extent, owing to the partial strengthening of sterling, and our imports would cost less. Production here in replacement of some imports would become viable. These favourable factors would allow us to eliminate the trade deficits. The benefits to the City of London would speed the process.

(c) Unemployment
All costs, as we have noted, are payments for services, productive or otherwise. The pay and price cuts would, therefore, strengthen the economy, increase the value of savings and cause a considerable reduction in unemployment. Purchasing power has to precede employment, so the gain by the service creditors would be the catalyst. Workers would be priced into, instead of out of, jobs. They would cease to be a burden on the state.

(d) The Pay and Price Structure

The object is not to create a low wage economy; it is simply to reduce the pay and price structure to the supportable level. Purchasing power in real terms would increase. Since pay cuts at the bottom are not envisaged, the low-paid would be better off. When the strengthening of the exchange rate ensued, it would probably be found that all British wages were above the level advocated in the social chapter. We could stop living like church mice!

(e) Shopfloor and Boardroom Rewards

The excessive disparities would be reduced, which can only be good for industrial relations. The additional jobs expected would remove the fear of unemployment and could make more overtime available. Trade unions could adopt policies more in keeping with their interests. Their members would share the benefits of scientific and technological advances, instead of chasing after illusory, and job-destroying, pay increases.

Application of the remedial measures

Now that pay increases recouped from higher prices have been shown to be the sole cause of inflation, we can consider some practicable ways of countering our economic problems. Clearly, we need some new rules to govern our industrial affairs and, for example, can no longer allow employers and employees to enter into agreements which debase the currency.

The economy is the result of the trading activity. Remedial measures must, therefore, ensure that this activity is conducted in the interests of the nation. Such a desirable situation can only be achieved at present by reducing pay and prices.

The inflationary process can be halted by a wage freeze, but more than that is needed to take care of our difficulties. One was tried, but, unfortunately, was coupled with other measures which were damaging, such as restrictions on bank lending. The real issue must not be fudged again and no sops can be given. Parties trade solely in services and only the values placed upon them can have any bearing.

That wage freeze was opposed and was deemed to have broken down. In fact, the wage addicts were allowed to have their way, instead of having their ailment treated.

In a logical extension of the wage-freeze principle, a government could obtain power to raise or lower wages in accordance with the needs of the nation, under a procedure which could for convenience be named 'The Wages Pound Scheme'.

Employers could be required to pay so much in the pound. Thus, if the government wanted to raise the wage level, it could insist on, say, 105p being paid for each pound of remuneration; similarly, if it wished to reduce the wage level, it could make the controlling figure, say, 95p per pound. We would then have a 'wages pound' as well as a normal one.

It would not be necessary to take action against prices. When wage cuts were implemented, there would not be enough purchasing power in the community to buy the available goods and services at current prices. Suppliers have to sell goods and services on a regular basis to sustain their cash flows and to keep within their borrowing limits. Otherwise, they become insolvent. They would know that the next production run or working period was going to cost less and they would have the immediate benefit of a reduction in their weekly or monthly wages bills. Both employers and the self-employed would be similarly affected.

The public would expect price reductions, and woe betide any party who did not introduce them. Those trying to maintain prices would have their business snapped up by competitors, because the same profits in real terms could be made with lower prices.

It would be necessary to provide an index of the purchasing power of the pound, so that everyone would see that its value was increasing and be able to check their own positions against it. Hopefully, that would establish confidence in, and support for, the remedial measures.

As an alternative, a policy could be introduced to force down prices. This, in turn, would oblige employers to cut pay, so the results would be similar. Discussions on the problem are, therefore, desirable with a view to finding the best way of enforcing the remedial measures.

Once the economy had been brought into the area of tolerance, further pay cuts would not be necessary. Maximum employment would exist and prices would be falling gently in reflection of the benefits of scientific and technological advances.

At this point, measures under the second phase are required to ensure that the inflationary malpractices are not allowed to recur. To this end, the government could bring in legislation entitled, say, 'The Remuneration Act' or 'The Protection of the Currency Act', under which increases in remuneration could only be paid from profits already earned and payments in kind were prohibited. This would ensure that employers already had the purchasing power to transfer to their employees.

In support of these measures, the Bank of England, as the regulatory authority, could instruct the commercial banks not to finance pay increases. Moreover, the government could oblige organisations increasing pay and/or dividends from profits to make equivalent *reductions* in prices and those incurring losses to cut pay and prices.

The benefits would then be shared with the rest of the community.

Just how far the measures have to go would be a matter of trial and error. Nevertheless, their implementation would be fair, simple, workable, effective and visible. Their nature confirms that inflation is a trading problem and not a monetary one.

Most of us have seen the hardship and worry which rising prices cause to elderly people on fixed incomes. This, too, is the future which faces the worker of today and redundancy can hasten that end. The proposed remedial measures are, therefore, in the general interests of the workforces and only those who have been taking excessive rewards would have their purchasing power cut back.

To have a system which creates poverty among the defenceless members of our society is a very poor reflection on us as a nation. Yet that is what wage inflation does. It should be realised, therefore, that there is no bottomless pool from which funds can be drawn for the payment of wages or any other rewards. The only true pool is the profits one. It represents the benefits of trading and these can be shared.

The disparity between shopfloor and boardroom rewards is not the only cause of inequity. Television, for example, has had a major impact on our lives and has made it possible for many people to earn sums out of all proportion to their contribution to the economy. It has upset the principle of the division of labour. How can the baker trade with the (. . . .) player? Do not ask me to reveal my own prejudices. Insert your own pet hate. Yet, which can we do without? Sound management of the economy demands that consideration be given to this growing problem. The top rewards should go to those who make the greatest contributions to the interests of the nation. Perhaps sport should pay to be televised, rather than the other way round.

Some further advantages arising from the remedial measures would be:

(1) Workers would have a vested interest in doing their best to ensure that their employers made profits.

(2) There would be no point in workers striking for more pay, at least until the end of the financial year. Disputes would then only involve the amounts to be awarded in pay increases and *taken from* prices.

(3) Businesses incurring losses would be unable to pay increased wages. Inefficient ones would lose workers to better run organisations. Those temporarily in difficulty would have the opportunity to make a quicker recovery.

(4) Investment would become more attractive.

(5) The pressure to debase the basic money supply, and the resulting inflation, would disappear.

(6) People on fixed incomes and those not employed in profit-making organisations would enjoy the rise in the standard of living in proportion to their income.

(7) Since the main suppliers of goods and services are bank borrowers, less lending would be needed to finance the present level of trading activity and a surplus would become available to finance growth. Further comment on this issue, and how it comes about, appears in the next section.

(8) It would not be difficult to enforce the remedial measures as organisations which account for most of the remuneration paid from profit-making activities have to produce audited accounts. The legislation could make provision for the auditors to check the pay

situation and, if in order, to certify that to the best of their knowledge and belief the stipulations had been observed.

A disadvantage would be that a number of service debtors would find that their financial positions were overextended and steps would need to be taken to reschedule their debts. This could be offset, at least partially, by more work and overtime becoming available.

Many executives have been made redundant, particularly aged between 50 and 60 years of age. In fairness, an effort must be made, when they want to work, to reinstate them at or near their previous levels.

A scheme like the Wages Pound one is needed to undo the harm caused by wage inflation and bad management decisions, to reduce unemployment quickly and to bring the pay and price level into the area of tolerance. It may be required for corrective purposes from time to time thereafter. The Remuneration Act could then be expected to provide stable and prosperous conditions beyond our experience.

The financing of the remedial measures

It is not enough to say that the remedial measures would result in (1) less lending being needed to finance the present level of trading activity and (2) a surplus becoming available to finance growth. The process must be demonstrated.

Basic money can only be created by debtor spending on creditor services and, in like manner, destroyed by the converse action. Cutting pay and prices would not, therefore, reduce the quantity of basic money; such action would increase the purchasing power of the pound. In consequence, the service credits would become more valuable and the service debts more burdensome to the same extent.

For example, a company with an overdraft of, say, £100,000 would still owe that sum, though in real terms the indebtedness would have increased. The cash flow, both in and out of the account, would be reduced, the former because of the price cuts and the latter due to lower expenditure.

Savers, however, would have an incentive to spend more, as

goods and services would have become cheaper. The trading activity would increase, more jobs would result, extra overtime would be necessary and the standard of living would rise. The increased business would make organisations more profitable, owing to the economies of size, and allow them to reduce their borrowing requirements. The released funds would become available to finance growth.

That is not all. The incoming cash flows, such as shops' takings and outstanding accounts, would come in at the old prices, while the benefits of pay cuts and new prices to be paid would be virtually immediate. The cash outflows would, therefore, fall before the inflows, advances would be reduced and more released funds would result.

What would be the effect on deposits? The incoming funds would be reduced, but so would the outgoing expenditure, so, *ceteris paribus*, the balances would be unchanged. Deposits and advances would now reflect the fact that the trading bias had been tipped in favour of the buyers at the expense of the sellers.

To clinch the argument, it is necessary to show that the same amount of basic money can be made to finance a greater amount of trading activity.

Assume that Jack owns a smallholding and employs Larry as a labourer. Each week, he gives his employee an IOU for £100 and gets it back in return for food, clothing and shelter. A drifter arrives in the neighbourhood and Jack sees an opportunity to improve his own standard of living. He informs Larry that from next week he will give him an IOU for £50 and charge this sum for the necessities. Then he takes on the drifter under a similar arrangement.

Jack is a fair man and does not believe that the economy runs best when everyone takes as much as they can out of it, so he improves his provision of food, clothing and shelter. The results are more employment and an all-round improvement in the standard of living. The same quantity of basic money is financing a greater amount of trading activity; the purchasing power of the pound has increased.

In this situation, Jack is a service debtor and basic money is created by the performance of services for him by his employees. It is destroyed when he meets their requirements.

Now, suppose instead that Jack was operating with an overdraft facility of £100 and used borrowed cash for the payments. Less lending is needed to finance Larry's transactions and a surplus has become available to cover those of the drifter or, in other words, growth. Larry and the drifter are using deposit accounts, the totals of which are unaffected by the change.

What can we learn? The settlement system must be designed to take care of the desired circumstances and not be allowed to act as a barrier. Jack can be said to be the government, monetary authority, economic establishment and business rolled into one. It can be seen that (1) employment is in the gift of the government; (2) the introduction of interest rates, and the tampering therewith, would be irrelevant; (3) practice does not accord with unilateral monetary theory; and (4) business and industry run the economy.

If Larry's position is strong enough, he might be able to prevent the drifter being taken on, thus confirming the cause of unemployment. His aspirations might lead him to believe that he can get more out of Jack for the same amount of work.

Another point of interest in the example is that Jack's little world is a separate monetary area. Further lessons to be learned from it are, therefore, that we need small separate monetary areas on which to experiment and must not tie our hands by joining a big one.

World price inflation

When world prices are increased and we are obliged to pay the higher sums demanded, we have to accept that the trading strengths of our suppliers have grown, while ours have correspondingly weakened. In other words, their standards of living have risen and ours has fallen. Such a situation must inevitably reflect in our spending power. Indeed, it shows up in a fall in the value of the pound and in higher prices at our retail outlets. The supportable pay and price level has gone down.

In these circumstances, the reaction of the workforces is to demand more pay to cover the increases in their costs of living. If granted, however, pay increases worsen the situation as corresponding sums have to be added to prices.

The beneficiaries of the pay increases would, of course, maintain their own financial positions at the expense of the rest of the community. Some wage earners, however, would be priced out of their jobs and some work would leave the country. The penalties are too high.

An increase in world prices has the same effect on our economy as an inflationary wage increase and should be dealt with in like manner. If it is a major event, we must use the Wages Pound Scheme to reduce our pay and price level.

A fall in world prices affects our economy in a similar manner to a pay and price cut. If then the economy is pushed from the area of tolerance into a deflationary position, the remedy is to use the Wages Pound Scheme to raise the pay and price level.

The oil crisis presented us with a problem at the time. Now that we know how to handle such an event, the impact should not be so great. We can offset the effects of increases and reductions in world prices and there is little reason why they should ever again be problems of moment.

When we start putting our own economy in order, it will become obvious to other nations that we have found the solution. They will copy our actions. This should lead to greater stability in the economies of the world.

9

The Challenge

Try to break the accounting formula

As, dear reader, you are no doubt now aware, my work is not based
on Keynesian concepts, monetarism or any other economic theories.
Indeed, my findings come purely from a consideration of trading
practices and the means by which they are settled. *Inter alia*, they
show that business and industry run the economy and not the
monetary authorities. The findings contrast starkly with traditional
teaching and the theoretical views deduced from empirical studies,
neither of which, it should be noted, is proved in any way.

Post-barter, every transaction has been settled in accordance with
the status rules. Indeed, it is, I believe, impossible to devise a
transaction which defeats them. As a result, the settlement systems
are mathematically precise and there can be no monetary phenomenon. In truth, the problems of the economy are not caused by the
monetary and banking systems; they lie solely with the terms of
trade, which translates into pay and prices.

My analysis is complete and proved to the hilt. Indeed, since the
publication of my first book – *The Monetary Analysis* – I have
simply found more and better ways of presenting my case. No one
has advanced any sound arguments in dispute of my contentions,
yet, if I am wrong, proof should not be difficult. One has only to find

a transaction, an event or an abuse which defeats the status rules and has all of economic history, post-barter, from which to choose!

The accounting formula, in its amended form, appears on page 74 and you, dear reader, are now challenged to find a way of breaking it. All I ask is that no one who fails this test will try unfairly to sweep my contentions aside. That, of course, would mean that the unsuccessful ones in academic circles and positions of authority would be obliged to reconsider respectively their teachings and practices.

This is a matter of national importance and not, for example, one of semantics. The benefits to be derived from correcting unilateral monetary theory would be enormous.

10

Observations

Conclusions

My first inclination was to give this chapter the title, 'Conclusions'. Then, I realised that I might be closing minds rather than opening them, in much the same way as unilateral monetary theory has done. I want my readers to consider, as far as possible, the implications of, and benefits to be gained from, bilateral monetary theory. Moreover, I look to them, where they can, to make their own contributions to the new knowledge.

That said, some conclusions are unavoidable. For example, the fundamental principles of basic money creation and destruction, governed by the status rules, are immutable. Nevertheless, developments will always take place in the trading activity and settlement systems. For that reason, the monetary authorities must always keep abreast of such changes and be ready to take action quickly against practices not considered to be in the national interest.

I have provided the foundation and the first few building blocks of bilateral monetary theory. My findings represent the extent to which I have travelled down a new road with exciting prospects. Nevertheless, I do not know where it eventually leads and cannot provide all the answers and conclusions. Here, however, are some observations from the position I have reached along the way.

Basic deposits

We have noted the differences between deposits and basic money. Gross deposits, therefore, consist of two parts, (1) basic deposits and (2) the rest. The former represent basic money supply credits on being paid in and are used to cover the spending of savers and borrowers, while the rest, collectively described as 'the froth', have no value other than that they are required by the double-entry book-keeping system. Ideally, therefore, for the purpose of measuring basic deposits, the rest should be deducted from the gross figures.

Fortunately, however, there is no need to measure the credits and debts of the basic money supply, as it is self-regulating. Moreover, its quantity is a reflection of the economy and not an influence on it. Thus, the important issue is to understand what is happening. We must not allow ourselves to be deceived into believing that all deposits are purchasing power. Remember that even basic deposits do not come into that category. Purchasing power is actually the part of deposits savers intend to spend plus the part borrowers have obtained for the same purpose.

When restrictions on bank lending were temporarily introduced, bank managers, who had been happy for prestige reasons to see both deposits and advances pushed up, were instructed to set off creditor and debtor balances in the same names. The restrictions were based on the misconception that bank lending created money and, if they had been effective, would have damaged the economy considerably. Luckily, the banks were able to avoid them and put themselves in a position where they could increase lending without breaking the rules to the extent of the balances set off.

History, as they say, repeats itself. Banks have been instructed to meet capital requirements, which increase in relation to their deposits. Now, they have noted that a large part of their foreign currency transactions result, in many cases, in their owing to, and being owed by, another bank credits and debts which can be netted. That puts them in the same position in relation to capital requirements as they were in respect of bank lending.

The basic deposits are of great importance and the lending of them has been a major factor in advancing the standards of living of nations. Consideration, however, needs to be given to supervising their use, as some forms of lending, such as for gambling, hedging, investment and overtrading, are not in the national interest and can result in damaging losses of basic money supply.

Markets have necessary functions to perform and it is desirable that they should be stable. Throwing funds at them by lending, especially for undesirable practices, can make them volatile. Such actions should, therefore, be prevented.

Accordingly, every step should be taken to ensure that the funds available for lending are put to the best use. They make up a limited resource.

The undesirable features of lending

Lending can be divided roughly into four categories, (1) Corporate finance, (2) Personal borrowing, (3) Facilities for speculation and (4) Government requirements.

The first is needed to finance the production of goods and services, including the basic needs of food, clothing and shelter; the second to allow people to live beyond their immediate means; the third to assist parties to 'make money'; and the fourth to enable the government to meet its responsibilities. Since the supply of deposits available for lending is limited, increases in any category crowd out borrowing elsewhere.

Categories (1) and (4) are the important ones and must be accommodated; category (2) should be strictly limited to surplus funds; and category (3) must be banned.

Corporate finance is normally provided and used responsibly. A watch, however, must be kept for overtrading. Examples of this are (1) companies taking on contracts too large for their resources and (2) excessive funds being made available for a particular purpose, such as those lent prior to the recent recession for building more office accommodation than was required.

In the past, when demand for personal borrowing has risen, interest rates have been put up, thereby, as we shall see in the next

section, adversely affecting the cost of living and causing bankruptcies and liquidations of businesses and industries. A housing market,
in which prices are rising, is not, therefore, healthy and appropriate
steps must be taken to limit the funds being made available to it.
The same principle applies to excessive hire purchase and even the
situation where rich people finance their affairs with bank borrowing. Personal borrowing must not be allowed to make corporate
finance more expensive or, for any reason, to achieve preference
over it.

I cannot speak out too strongly against any form of lending for
speculative purposes. As I have already said, I have no objection to
parties using their own or collected funds for such purposes, but that
does not apply to borrowed ones. It is difficult, of course, to assess
the extent to which such facilities are being provided, but it should
be noted that they can, for example, (1) push up the prices of stocks
and shares and (2) enable major foreign currency speculators to take
on, and defeat, governments. Borrowed funds should not be thrown
at any market, but this particularly applies to those engaged in
gambling. This may, or may not, be a problem at present, but if it is,
the borrowing must be eliminated and, if it is not, steps should be
taken to ensure that it does not become one.

Any reduction in the cost of borrowing is, of course, beneficial
to the government, so it should be looking for better ways of
managing the economy than the faulty interest rate transmission
mechanism.

The interest rate transmission mechanism

Alterations in the Bank of England's base interest rates, to be
effective, would need to cause a material number of parties to
change their behaviour. Thus, increases should damp down the
demand for borrowing and reductions should cause it to pick up.

Personally, I have never made a decision based on the interest rate
changes, so I must ask you, dear reader, some relevant questions.
Have you ever been put off purchasing anything, say, from a small
item to a house, by an increase in interest rates or decided to buy

something because they have fallen? Do you know of anyone who has? Are you aware of any firm or company where the criterion for a purchasing decision was an interest rate change? In my opinion, the answers would almost invariably be, 'No'. I think, therefore, that the monetary authorities should ask for any such cases where the answer is, 'Yes' to be referred to them. After all, knowledge, rather than theory, should be the basis of their decisions.

It is true that the upward changes would make goods and services more expensive and the downward ones would have the opposite effect, so the questions have to be asked again. This time a consolidated one will suffice. Do you, your firm, company or group buy fewer goods and services when prices are raised, and more in the reverse circumstances? I believe that the answers in most cases would be covered by statements to the effect that it is not necessary to watch prices to that extent and buying decisions are made on desire to purchase rather than price. The exceptions are, of course, people with limited means and businesses verging on insolvency. Increases in interest rates force the poor to buy less, bankrupt weak businesses, cause unemployment and add to the burdens on the state. That means that interest rate increases are a cruel and unacceptable way to curb the wrong part of demand; this is particularly so when logic tells us that demand is healthy and, along with need, should be accommodated; more trading activity is highly desirable. The authorities cannot curb the demand of the rich and the comfortable.

The verdict must be that increases in interest rates are, in the main, irrelevant, but, in their limited effectiveness, are extremely harmful. The monetary authorities must, therefore, look for other, fairer and more efficient ways of eliminating the really undesirable features in the economy. Blanket practices, such as tampering with interest rates, simply will not do.

Once facilities for speculation are banned, the need will be to prevent personal borrowing crowding out corporate finance. It should now be appreciated that the housing boom inflicted damage on our manufacturing industry, when the over-financed personal demand forced up interest rates.

I do not wish to judge the monetary authorities too harshly, as their practices are based on the false notions of unilateral monetary theory. There will, however, be no excuse for them if they do not change their ways. I trust, therefore, that they will now consider the remedial measures which I have proposed, and any other helpful suggestions others may be able to make.

Aims of economic policy

The top aims of economic policy are full employment and stable prices. Personally, I would go further than this and couple the first factor with falling prices. That should be the result of properly applying the benefits of scientific and technological advances.

A brief look at economic history may be helpful, bearing in mind that the viewpoints are based on an inadequate definition of 'money' and false unilateral monetary theory.

In the 19th century, the prevailing opinion was that economies were regulated by the market forces. Upturns were prompted by low wages and prices, while downturns ensued in the reverse circumstances. On balance, inflation was virtually absent and prices comparatively stable. My comment would be that the sellers were not sufficiently organised to prevail in the market-place, a situation which was altered by the formation of trade unions at the beginning of the 20th century.

The lengthy depression and prevalent unemployment before the Second World War made the market forces theory untenable and led to the notion that governments should intervene. It was proposed that demand should be managed; thus, it would be encouraged by government spending on public works, cutting taxes and lowering interest rates and would be discouraged by less spending, more taxes and higher interest rates. A small amount of inflation was deemed necessary to stimulate the economy. I take the view that intervention was, and is, necessary, but regard the methods – fiscal policy – as inappropriate. Demand should be accommodated and not curbed.

Inflation was allowed to become a serious problem. The short flirtation with incomes policy, in so far as it related to pay, was a step in the right direction, but monetarism soon took over instead. The view that inflation could be controlled by manipulating the growth of 'money' came into vogue. Since inflation is not a monetary problem and there was no proper definition of 'money', it is hardly surprising that monetarism has proved ineffective. Business and industry – market forces – were allowed a free hand, with the results we have already noted. It is quite wrong to credit any favourable movements in the economy to monetarism.

The latest policy is to have a target rate for inflation of $2^1/_2$ per cent and attempt control of demand by tampering with the interest rates. It has no bearing on our real problems, but appears to be working because business and industry operate nowadays in a very competitive world and fear of unemployment is curbing inflationary pay claims. The benefits of scientific and technological advances are, however, going to the sellers.

The foregoing are all blanket policies and are unsuitable on those grounds alone. Coupled with their many other faults, they must now be consigned to history and suitable policies based on bilateral monetary theory introduced instead.

Unilateral monetary theory

Such theory is focused inwards instead of outwards. It is based on the false notion that 'money' is a single item, which acts as a medium of exchange, a unit of account and a store of value. Virtually all intelligent thought devoted to the subject has been directed into trying to make the impossible work.

In truth, basic money is a credit in services of one party and a debt in services of another. Consequently, a factor consisting of two separate sides cannot properly be represented by a single item, nor can its properties be transferred to a title (medium of exchange) or a measure (unit of account).

Will reason now prevail or should I use shock tactics by saying that unilateral monetary theory is a compilation of erudite nonsense based on false premises?

Indoctrination

Unilateral monetary theory is in a sorry state. Our universities are teaching false concepts, the monetary authorities are basing their practices on unsound principles and the endless repetition by the media of the incorrect views ensures that no one escapes the indoctrination.

Universities

The errors we have discussed are on a massive scale and it is a formidable task to put them to rights. Moreover, it is a quantum leap from establishing the true nature of 'money' to the acceptance of the principles of demand and need accommodation. Nevertheless, I have taken the first steps. I trust that our universities will now correct their teachings and reconstruct monetary theory on a sound foundation.

Perhaps they could introduce crash courses to cure the indoctrination and arrange for the basic principles of bilateral monetary theory to be taught in schools.

Monetary authorities

All monetary measures are based, at present, on unrealistic fears, such as of inflation or overheating, and are designed to curb the economy. On these grounds alone, they should be abandoned. Again, however, it can be noted that the main objections are that they are based on misconceptions and do not deal with our real problems.

At present, credence is being given to forecasts based on the monetary aggregates comprising false money supply. Forecasts are only needed for events, which are outwith our control, and that situation should no longer exist. By managing the pay and price structure, we should be able to drive the economy in whatever direction is desired.

I am saddened to note that the Bank of England is not regarded as the pre-eminent central bank. It still performs its functions as part of the banking system in an exemplary fashion, but it has been advocating and applying measures, however ineffectively, based on false monetary theory, as also has the Treasury.

All the central banks seem to be basing their actions on the same false premises. In consequence, in free countries economies are run by business and industry. As a result, they always function to a major extent, though the national interest is not the prime consideration. Such shortcomings need to be addressed.

In this connection, I am of the opinion that the reputation of the Bundesbank as a more competent monetary authority than the Bank of England is based on myths; the simple fact is that German business and industry have outperformed ours.

The government

The monetary authorities have been imagining that they have been beneficially influencing the economy by altering the interest rates. As a result, the government's economic policies have been too negative and have left too much to chance. Now, it should take practical, as opposed to theoretical, control of the economy and stop relying on the advocates of unsound unilateral monetary theory.

It could start immediately by passing the proposed law requiring organisations increasing pay and/or dividends to take an equivalent sum from prices. Pay in this context includes all forms of remuneration and the value of perquisites, the stock option type of which should be banned.

Such a law would have a dramatic effect in reducing and preventing inflation. Moreover, it would enable the government to dispense with the regulators of the privatised utilities, since it would be a better way of curbing monopolistic practices. It deserves a name, say, 'The Payback Law'.

It is quite absurd to believe that economic policies must be of a hairshirt nature and that an 'iron Chancellor' is required. 'If it is not hurting, it is not working' is a false notion. The economy provides our rising standard of living and anything which hurts it, or us, can only be damaging.

The Chancellor's duties

As I see it, the main duties of the Chancellor of the Exchequer are to raise essential revenue and to protect the value of the pound. A small amount of inflation, or a target figure in that area, is not, therefore, acceptable.

Cutting taxes, too, is not logical as a continuing policy and even worse is the granting of tax relief, particularly when based on false premises. It is, of course, correct for the government to seek value for its expenditure, but this should be the limits of its efforts in that direction.

Many issues cannot be left to business and industry, as they are not, in the short term, economic propositions; they should be financed by the government for the purposes of keeping abreast of advances and reaping future rewards.

We can add a third duty to those of the Chancellor – to ensure the growth of the economy. Fortunately, it has become possible for this duty to be carried out by efficient management of the pay and price structure.

Such action would alleviate poverty, as those on low incomes would benefit from the remedial measures. Moreover, the government would eventually be in a strong enough position to consider negative income tax and the elimination of poverty could become possible.

What a contrast there is between such a policy and the trivial one of tampering with the interest rates. Low interest rates occur when trading activity falls and the demand for borrowing is down; high interest rates can be charged when trading activity rises and the demand for borrowing is up. The authorities do not really control the rates and are obliged to follow the market forces. There is, therefore, no justification for giving credit for favourable movements in the economy to changes in the interest rates.

Claiming the credit for getting inflation down, even if justified, would not really be an achievement; it would simply be a lesser failure. Inflation has to be eliminated along with the buyers' disadvantage.

Politicians

Politicians should not seek general advice from economists. They should tell them specifically what they want and ask how their requirements can be met. For example, they might say that they need a policy which will ensure full employment, falling prices, stable interest rates and economic growth. They could tell their advisers to devise such a policy or come back with their resignations!

Because they have this principle the wrong way round, they have been led to believe that full employment is out of reach and yet they still expect us to vote for them on the grounds that they cannot cure our problems!

Commercial bankers

Bank lending has been a great boon to the human race and has enabled the achievement of standards of living which, without it, would have been well out of reach. Moreover, the banking systems have been honed by generations of bankers, whose expertise seems to have baffled the economists. Those systems, however, are simply means of settlement and, as such, are entirely neutral. Consequently, it is actions influencing the terms of trade, and not monetary measures, which are required.

Bankers should learn to fight their corner and defend their practices. Perhaps then they would be held in better public esteem and not be blamed for problems not of their making. They have no reason to be ashamed and indeed are entitled to considerable credit!

Trade unions

The market forces are between buyers and sellers, and not between employers and employees. Indeed, the last-named two are both sellers and agreements between them cannot be expected to produce a viable pay and price structure.

Every year, scientific and technological advances make it easier and cheaper for the economy to meet our needs. Pay increases, offset by productivity, result in the benefits of such advances going solely to the workforces instead of to the public in general.

Worse still, those recouped from higher prices debase the currency, devalue savings, price out the weaker buyers, cause trade deficits, increase poverty, create unemployment and, paradoxically, result in a low wage economy.

The trade unions should, therefore, support the proposal to cut pay, not at the bottom but progressively thereafter, with the stipulation that the savings in costs be deducted from prices.

The media

Some economists have ready access to the media and a few have had their views strongly supported by it. This can result in mere opinion being hyped into unsound doctrine of the 'everybody knows' category. All views, however eminent their advocates may be, are challengeable and only those which can be proved should be accepted.

The media should be more ready to give space to those who express views challenging the establishment. No one does this lightly and the media are the only outlets of real consequence through which a hearing can be gained. All new ideas, in whatever field, come from single minds and start as one person's opinion against the established views. In spite of the odds, that opinion is sometimes right.

Modern technology

Modern technology is being introduced at a fast pace in the monetary and banking systems. Nevertheless, the basic situation demonstrated in the example of A and B is unalterable and will always apply to the trading activity. Everything else post-barter, from the use of cowrie shells to the newest means of settlement, is simply a development which has made the dealings of the As and Bs of this world, whether as individuals or groups, more convenient and more efficient. Thus, they are still the ones who create and destroy basic money.

Unemployment

We have established that the pay and price structure in Britain is too high. Owing to the avarice of managements and the aspirations of the workers, there is continuous pressure of varying degrees to increase pay and perquisites on the one hand and prices on the other. This is the cause of unemployment. Thus, the workforces debase the currency, price some of their peers out of their jobs, prevent others from being engaged on account of the high cost and ensure that the economy underperforms. They do not, however, have it all their own way, for the unemployed are obliged to become a burden on the state or, in other words, the taxpayers. The workforces should realise, therefore, that responsible behaviour in accepting pay and price cuts would take a load from their shoulders.

There is no shortage of possible jobs. The needs of the poor have to be met, major projects are in the pipeline, more desirable research can be pursued, provision can be made for additional health care and a higher level of trading activity is within reach. All that is lacking is finance.

Now that we have a method of providing extra funds, the opportunity is open to us to cure unemployment permanently.

A further benefit would arise from the social consequences. People are much more likely to be good citizens if they can obtain jobs within the system than if they are excluded from it.

London money markets

The Bank of England is introducing measures to change the ways it operates in the money markets These will not alter the underlying principles. Thus, cash will continue to flow in the opposite direction to government debt to mop up surpluses and to relieve shortages.

The discount houses, however, will largely lose their privileged position and the Bank will trade a greater variety of government debt with a growing number of financial organisations.

These new practices will put the United Kingdom on a similar footing to other countries in the European Union.

An independent 'economiciary'

The mystery of the vanishing money supply and the accounting formula prove that the economic profession have erred on a massive scale. No doubt they will try to defend their positions, but the sooner they realise their cause is lost, the better it will be for all of us. Unsound policies based on their fallacies have been put into practice, while the necessary management of the pay and price structure has been dismissed out of hand.

Many 'think-tanks' and review bodies have been set up, but, without a sound basis for their deliberations, fail to deal with our real problems. Productivity is supposed to ensure that pay can be increased, while prices remain stable. Yet, consideration is continually being given to granting one group or another, productive or otherwise, pay increases often in excess of the rate of inflation. When will it be realised that these review bodies are being asked to decide to what extent the groups under discussion should be allowed to debase the currency?

The economy needs overall management to give it proper direction, to protect it from excesses and to make it conform to the national interest. Business and industry have already disqualified themselves from these responsibilities due to their managements feathering their own nests and ruthlessly dispensing with 'redundant' employees, while the Treasury and the Bank of England are too deeply indoctrinated by false unilateral monetary theory. In any event, these institutions are participants in the economy and have specific practical duties to carry out. It is undesirable, therefore, that they should be both players and referees.

In addition, it has to be recognised that the economy is developing in directions we have not seen before. Indeed, all sorts of ways are being devised to obtain benefits from modern technology and to exploit the paying public. Such buyers are more than ever in need of protection.

Many of the highest incomes being paid in the City of London are in respect of jobs which can only properly be described as forms of gambling. Questions must, therefore, be asked in relation to the sizes of the operations involved and to what extent finance is being provided in support of the activities. We must not allow desirable and necessary lending to be crowded out by facilities to finance gambling or excessive salaries.

The need for management of the economy has grown in step with the developments and the current practices are clearly inadequate to cope with them. They do not deal, as we have seen, with our real problems nor the inequalities arising therefrom.

The notion that the economy can be taken out of the political sphere is naive, as it covers the whole ambit of human affairs. Policy recommendations should, therefore, come from bodies specifically set up to deal with them. Personally, I take the view that the issues are now on too large a scale to be handled by the Treasury and the Bank of England. Accordingly, the government might consider setting up a commission to advise on the management of the economy.

It is, of course, envisaged that the accumulated mythology presently masquerading as monetary theory would be discarded. The members of the commission would, therefore, have to be fully versed in bilateral monetary theory and to have faith in it.

Major issues affecting the economy would fall to be referred to the commission, initially by the government and later by the public, for consideration and recommendations. Obvious ones are the pay and price structure, the disparities between shopfloor and boardroom rewards, excessively high salaries in financial services, the effects of television on incomes and the various perquisites. These are all factors disturbing the principles of the division of labour, under which we trade with one another.

The question of poverty would be a matter for reference to the commission and ways must be sought of alleviating it. The fact that the poor form considerable percentages of the populations of developed nations shows that they are not being adequately represented, or protected, by the present systems.

In the meantime, the government should consider what steps it could take to this end itself. For example, since savings always equal borrowings and have no special merit, the Peps and Tessa schemes could be cancelled. It is quite wrong for tax relief to be granted, when there is no benefit to the economy and there are much greater needs elsewhere. Most people have simply moved part of their existing savings into the schemes and, knowing the facts, many might now feel that they should take them back out.

The merit wrongly attached to savings is, of course, widespread. Thus, it is believed that the 'tiger' economies perform better than the western ones, because they have higher ratios of savings to gross domestic products. It should be noted, however, that cutting pay and prices would result in savings remaining unchanged, while the cost of the gross domestic product would fall. In other words, the savings ratio would rise. A low savings ratio simply shows that the workforces are overpaid. It would be part of the commission's duties to rid us of the misconceptions arising from false unilateral monetary theory.

Inter alia, the recommendations of the commission could give the country a code of monetary practice, a greater sense of right and wrong and an end to extreme materialism. If successful, the commission might develop into a new institution – an independent 'economiciary'. It would be for the government to decide whether or not to accept its recommendations.

Central Banks

In the normal course of events, we ought to be able to rely on the central banks to follow policies which are in the best interests of their economies. This, however, is not the case at present.

The Bank of England has a fixed target rate for inflation and believes that it can achieve this objective by altering interest rates to curb demand. We have already noted that demand should not be curbed and that, in any event, the Bank cannot curb the demand of the rich and the comfortable, but only of the poor and the hard-pressed.

The Bundesbank relies on the quantity of broad money as an indicator of the likely course of future inflation and alters interest rates in the belief that it is thereby controlling the situation. We have seen that, if a country becomes cashless, borrowers use their holdings to reduce their advances and part of the broad money supply disappears; moreover, if banks were abolished, only a comparatively small part of deposits could be paid out in cash. Basing policy on money supply which largely does not exist, hardly inspires confidence and the objections to the interest rate adjustments are again valid. The severe level of unemployment in Germany can be read as evidence of what happens when a central bank is influenced by monetarism and allows real problems to go unaddressed. Unemployment, after all, is caused by the workforces insisting on being overpaid.

We need a yardstick by which economies can be judged. Here is mine. Scientific and technological advances taken in isolation continually enable us to meet our basic needs plus a few luxuries more easily and should result in falling prices, increased demand and full employment. No central bank fares well, when judged on that basis.

The Federal Reserve has recently (September 1997) expressed doubts about the precise definition of inflation and is allowing itself to be distracted by so-called asset-price inflation. Goods are a by-product of the system of trading in services and subsequent dealings in them are a form of barter, cash being one of the items exchanged. The status rules apply, but such dealings are of little importance, as the performance of services is not involved.

Inflation is a varying bias in the terms of trade favouring the service debtors, nothing more and nothing less. Can one be more precise than that? It belongs solely to the system of trading in services.

It must be clear now to readers that there is no hope of the economic profession or the monetary authorities recovering from their self-indoctrination without outside help. Monetarism has been accepted as a panacea, which would avoid the need for unpopular fiscal policy or the controversial earnings kind. It enjoys, and will continue to enjoy, the same level of success as the alchemists who sought to turn base metals into gold.

Disillusionment with it has to come; let us then anticipate it and look instead at the benefits to be gained from an earnings policy.

Managing the pay and price structure

The plight of the poor is the subject of endless commentary, continuous reports and high-sounding reviews. Nevertheless, the percentage of people in the category continues to rise. Very little concrete or immediate action is being, or has been, taken to relieve the poverty.

True, value added tax on fuel was reduced; it should be noted, however, that the government also gave up the share of the tax paid by the rest of the population. Who suffers most when the government loses income? The poor.

Cutting pay and prices is the cure for inflation, but it also alleviates poverty, increases demand, allows more business to be financed by the same amount of lending and reduces unemployment. If there is a panacea, this surely is it. The benefits to the poor would be dramatic and immediate. This, dear reader, is therefore a step which, no matter the reservations, simply must be taken. It is anticipated, of course that the cuts would be made in the progressive manner previously described.

Next, we have to consider ways of increasing the purchasing power of the low-paid. Introducing a minimum rate of pay is not the answer. It would cause a general increase in inflation, as all the differentials would be increased in step and the cost would be added to prices. Some unemployment would result and the poor people with no earnings would be worse off. The number of people creating inflation would rise, while the number causing deflation would fall. The correct remedy again is to cut pay, not at the bottom, but progressively thereafter, and insist on the savings being deducted from prices.

Wage claims are continually made, but, in present circumstances, few claimants know for what they are asking. There is no pool of funds, from which additional pay can be drawn. Indeed, the funds have to be diverted from their existing uses. The question to be asked, therefore, is at whose expense should a pay claim be met?

We all know that there is no such thing as a free lunch. Equally, there can never be a free health service or free education. There is always a beneficiary and a benefactor.

In the same way there is no such thing as a pay increase which does not have repercussions. Suppose that the government raises the pay of doctors working for the National Health Service. It must either recoup the cost from increased taxation or increase its borrowing. The first action reduces deposits, while the second increases advances. Either way, some existing borrowers are 'crowded out' of their facilities.

Trade unions have discovered that the price of pressing endless claims is unemployment and have moderated their demands. They have not yet realised that the real need is to claw back excessive remuneration, perquisites and dividends.

In the same vein, since basic money is subject to continuous creation and destruction, it is not readily available to be 'thrown' at problems. Instead, therefore, of thinking of using more 'money' for such difficulties, we have to arrange for more people to be employed in dealing with them.

Disparities between shopfloor and boardroom rewards are already a source of concern. Moreover, the speed at which incomes in the fields of entertainment, sport and other high-earning businesses are increasing, has become alarming. Even more so are the excessive salaries being paid in the City of London for activities which are nothing more than forms of gambling, dressed up euphemistically as dealings and investments. There is some justification for introducing specific pay and price cuts in all these cases, while using the

Payback Law to control the orderly market activities and to prevent future excesses.

The overall effect of the pay and price proposals would be to provide a degree of stability and equity. Doctors and judges, for example, would not find themselves falling behind and even our members of Parliament might be allowed to receive a fair level of remuneration!

We are all supposedly equal before the law. Why then should we allow some people to debase the currency and create further difficulties for the poor and the hard-pressed?

Miscellaneous points

There is a constant need to emphasise the differences between financial and material wealth. Goods, as we have noted, are a by-product of the system of trading in services and, in this regard, can never be more than media of exchange. That is why any form of them can be used in this way. Nominal money, virtually a substitute commodity, is simply a device which performs this function in the most efficient manner.

Such money, remember, is not a medium of exchange for goods *and* services, but for services only. Often we have to defer to common practice, but this is one case in regard to which we can no longer make such a concession. The sooner we correct the practice, the easier it will be for us to achieve full understanding of the nature of 'money'.

In like vein, we must stop talking of printing 'money'. Nominal money can be printed; basic money can only be created by debtor spending on creditor services.

It has, of course, been maintained wrongly that banks create money by lending; indeed, it has even been contended that they have done so to such an extent that they could have more than repaid the National Debt with the proceeds! The National Debt is the debtor balance of the country's current account and can only be reduced by, say, the proceeds of taxation or the rewards for the performance of services by the government.

I believe that I have shown that appropriate intervention in the economy is essential; it should, however, be kept to a minimum and should be consistent. It is wrong, for example, to have, in the longer term, regulators for some industries and not for others; equally, it is unjust to have restrictions on pay levels in the public sector, but not in the private one.

Clearly, there are already a large number of issues which could be referred to the proposed 'economiciary' for discussion and recommendations.

A more equitable society

The view that the economy works best if everyone tries to take as much as they can out of it is no longer tenable; indeed, the need is for everyone to contribute as much as they can to it. The strong have to carry the weak. They should accept that being able to do more than their share is a reward in itself and does not always require monetary recognition.

Clearly, we are much more interdependent than previously realised and a more equitable society should be devised to take account of this factor. Capitalism has much to commend it, but it can, and must, be made fairer.

We need to change our behaviour to that end. A growing economy, an absence of inflation, full employment, falling prices and a rising standard of living all round could then be our rewards – provided always we do not lose our sovereignty by agreeing to European Monetary Union.

Such are the prospects offered to us by bilateral monetary theory.

11

'The Monetary Analysis'

I was agreeably surprised to find that my above-mentioned book has stood a test of time in that there is very little of the text I need, or wish, to change. A few comments, however, would seem appropriate.

The descriptions 'creditor' and 'debtor' in that book and in this one are used in their normal senses and, of course, refer to obligations in cash terms. As, however, my definition of 'money' is a 'credit in services of one party and a debt in services of another', it is necessary to have distinguishing descriptions for the parties. In *The Monetary Analysis* I chose 'creditor party' and 'debtor party' for the purpose, whereas now I have adopted the more explicit 'service creditor' and 'service debtor'.

I had two forms of obligation, one in services and the other in cash. In *The Monetary Analysis* I tried to solve this problem by making the former 'money' and the latter a 'monetary instrument'. The distinction is clear enough, but one reader pointed out that it was too much to ask the public to change its centuries-old perception of money. I readily accept this point and have now selected 'basic (or real) money' for the former and 'nominal money' for the latter. Some form of consensus will, of course, eventually prevail.

In regard to the flows of funds, I wrote (page 27) that 'money circulates', but it has become clear that this situation should have been explained more specifically. Basic money is subject to a process of continuous creation and destruction in accordance with the status rules and can only be spent once; in terms of these parameters, therefore, it does not circulate. When, however, it has been created and the service credits deposited with banks, they can be passed on by lending and return to these organisations as new deposits or repayments of indebtedness. This is an entirely different process and does not change the quantity of basic money. Accordingly, it is more accurate to say that banks circulate, recirculate or rent out basic money supply credits, rather than that 'money circulates'.

On page 117, I wrote, 'Money is created, when a debtor party purchases shares from a creditor one – debtor spending on creditor services'. The corollary, of course, is that money is destroyed when a creditor party purchases shares from a debtor one – creditor spending on debtor services. The introduction of the accounting formula has enabled me to show that allowance in these statements must be made for the direct investment element. Transactions in stocks and shares are dealings in company debt; the debts are fixed at the times incurred and are still outstanding, but the subsequent prices paid for them vary.

The Monetary Analysis was published by The Book Guild Limited at some personal expense and is out of print. Some copies are, however, available from Messrs. A. L. Fleming, 12, Salisbury Road, Bromley, Kent. BR2 9PY. (Tel no 0181 313 0350).

In comparison with *Bilateral Monetary Theory*, its value lies in having many more book-keeping examples, though it does not have the accounting formula for the basic money supply.

Index

(See Contents for Chapters and Sections)